Screaming Without a Sound

Gracelyn Castle

Order this book online at www.trafford.com
or email orders@trafford.com

Most Trafford titles are also available at major online book retailers.

Note for Librarians: A cataloguing record for this book is available from Library
and Archives Canada at www.collectionscanada.ca/amicus/index-e.html

Printed in Victoria, BC, Canada.

ISBN: 978-1-4269-1927-5 (sc)

ISBN: 978-1-4269-1928-2 (dj)

Library of Congress Control Number: 2009939095

*Our mission is to efficiently provide the world's finest, most comprehensive book publishing
service, enabling every author to experience success. To find out how to publish your
book, your way, and have it available worldwide, visit us online at www.trafford.com*

Trafford rev. 11/23/2009

www.trafford.com

North America & international
toll-free: 1 888 232 4444 (USA & Canada)
phone: 250 383 6864 ♦ fax: 812 355 4082

This book is dedicated to my Baby Bird and Honey Bee
I love you more than words can say

There are so many people that I owe so much to that it would be impossible to thank all of my heroes. There have been many supporters in my life who have tried to lead, encourage, and cheer me on to victory and, although it may have taken years, they never gave up on me.

Thank you mom.

I wish to thank Debbie and Kathy. They spent countless hours reading my rough drafts, making suggestions, and just talking with me about it that I couldn't have written such a profound book without their help and support.

I also wish to thank Beatrice and Barbara. They cannot see the results of their hard work, but I know they are aware of everything they gave me.

Thank you to Elizabeth, Fred, Donald, Kathryn, Wayne, Adam, Nicole, Gary, Megan, Debra, Brad, Jeff, Greg, Patricia, and Melissa. You've been there and supported me through the best and worst, and for that, I will never be able to repay you or show you the extent of my gratitude. Thank you to Frank and Leslie for learning to love me.

Thank you Dr. B for leading me in the right direction. Thank you Dr. M for practically saving my life. They ALL challenged me to recover, supported me through the process, and rejoiced with me as I made it through my journey.

Thank you Samantha for reaching for the stars and not letting go of your dreams. Thank you Joshua and EllaGrace. You are the loves of my live. You are my babies, my heart, my love!

Most importantly, I wish to thank God. He saved me from myself. I owe everything to Him.

Prologue

If you choose to write a biography, the most logical place to start is the beginning. New beginnings offer hope after all, right? With this in mind, I wasn't even sure where my beginning started. My beginning of life was simple, but the beginning of becoming who I am wasn't always so easy to interpret. My life unfolds as a story, but the definitive beginning of who I was, and who I wanted to be wasn't clear. Was it when I was born – due to genetics? Was it the result of an early childhood molestation, or being the teenage victim of rape? Was it due to happen, perhaps, as I realized that I was different from other children? Did it unfold when my abusive broken marriage began to collapse? Was it the only night I spent away from my children – in jail – what set it off? Endings mark the end of one period and the beginning of another. It seemed like it had been so long since I had been happy that I really needed to know what was my new beginning so that I could look forward to the hope and happiness that it would offer. Was my experience in jail the beginning, since it is what led me to seek help? How could I dream of the hope offered by a new beginning if I couldn't even determine the ending of my pain and the new beginning of my hope. I wanted a new beginning. I wanted the hope it offered.

After many haunting memories, thoughts, and conclusions, I've realized that I have had a lot of beginnings. We all have, but mine have always been a little off key. I've realized that my beginnings are like many others; diversified, speckled with good and bad; but no matter what, my beginnings will always be touched by my mental illnesses. What I claim to now be my most important New Beginning is when I discovered my own pain, lost complete control of everything, spiraled downward, and felt the smallest inner voice telling me to not let go.

I needed something to get me through the minutes, hours, days…just something to help me hang on from one moment to the next, so "don't let go" became somewhat a mantra for me. Granted, sometimes it was during a low, but even such a simple reminder to oneself can help you get through the moment. I held on, learned about mental illness, still struggle, and believe that my true beginning was when I clutched the edge, climbed back out, and didn't let go. That's when I started becoming the person I wanted to be. I sought help, really figured out who I was, and am confident with the person I have become. I will always have my highs and lows, medication changes, and everything else that comes along with any other illness, but I can finally say that for now I am happy.

I cannot necessarily tell my story in a timeline order because my story is like a puzzle. Puzzles are generally completed randomly. The analogy reminds me of my life because my story is linked together by experiences and memories, more than years. Similar to the way puzzle pieces are linked together. It seems like my biggest mental illness landmarks and milestones or my extraordinary highs or lows connect my memories, without as much recall to the time or the year. Throughout my story you will find poems that I have written over the years, memorable moments I've gratefully experienced during my life so far that seemed untouched by mental illness, and horrific glimpses of what someone can suffer after abuse or due to a mental illness. When it comes to my life puzzle, it will definitely be completed out of order. Then again, maybe I don't have all the pieces. Maybe I never will. Maybe my pieces won't ever fit completely but I love the person I am becoming so there is always hope.

I will admit that I will have to embrace, endure, accept, and be fearful of some of the new beginnings in the future because, sometimes, I still wonder, will I ever let go? I'm happy, healthy, confident, and on the way to becoming the person I had hoped to become and when I wonder about my future stability, I can remind myself that there is always hope. Although the telling of my life story may begin with the years when I was an adult, readers will also feel my pain and differences that started much earlier, as they later read and follow the story of my childhood. Once I reached my mental illness stopping points, I had to search my past, make connections to how I felt then and now, and try to move forward. In order to put my life and memories on paper, I had to think, follow, and lead myself back in time from an adult to a child to recognize my new beginning. "Don't walk behind me, I may not lead. Don't walk in front of me, I may not follow. Just walk beside me and be my friend" as I try to complete my puzzle and help any other friend I have out there who may have felt like me.

For the protection and respect of others included in my life story, all names of people and places have been changed.

Mental Illness: The Truth Hurts

It doesn't matter time or place,
the day, the month, the year.
The name, the face, they're all the same
and all will end with fears and tears.
The rules of the game will never change,
but the players will pass with time
Each taking a piece of our shared pain along,
as a souvenir of the overwhelming quest they tried.

Age 27

We all try to beat mental illness, but is complete recovery even possible? I hold onto hope and haven't let go yet because I know continued recovery is always possible.

CHAPTER I

When You've Lost It All, What's Left To Be Taken?

The day I gave an offer to purchase our house was such a nerve wracking, yet exciting moment. The day the final foreclosure papers came barely two years later, it was a relief. What a difference a few years can make!

Ryan, my husband at the time, and I married just prior to my college graduation so we didn't want to purchase a house until I had a job. We knew I would be able to easily get one with my degrees, but we wanted the assurance of paychecks before making any financial commitments. It took us a few years, but we finally found a cute, small, and cozy home with three bedrooms and two and a half bathrooms. It also had a fenced in backyard and a garage. We paid way too much for it, but standing in the kitchen of our new home signing the papers made us both feel so grown up. We felt like we ruled the world then. Finally, we had something to call our own.

We decorated our son Taylor's room in eccentric colors and

racecars since that was his latest interest. Since my stepdaughter Noel finally had a room to herself we let her pick her decorations. She chose a surfer girl theme in beautiful blue and green tones. She had a knack for decorating, I must say. During this time, even though I didn't have a name for it yet, my bipolar disorder roller coaster and borderline personality disorder tendencies altogether were driving me insane! My anxieties were off the charts, even though I should have been celebrating more over such a great milestone. I was always a glass half empty person by nature, so in combination with my other mental illnesses, my anxiety was constantly increasing. I worried about the house, the kids, myself, my career, dangers in life, and even simplistic things like what to wear or what to cook, how to drive or order food; my anxiety was finally all consuming and had completely encompassed my life.

I would be in mania, and would stay awake for days painting, replacing, unpacking, decorating, and scatter-brained cleaning and all the while praising myself for how great I was at doing it and how useless everyone else was. Suddenly the next day or so I would be so depressed that I wouldn't even change out of my pajamas and would hate everyone else for not even caring. I would love the house because I was the one who found it, and the next day I'd be cursing Ryan because I hated one part or another of the house. I never felt stable. I never felt like myself because I couldn't even figure out who that was. I would look in the mirror, realize how fat I was, and commit myself to days without eating or binging and purging. Depending on my mood, I easily switched from one to the other. It was either all or nothing. High or low. Nonetheless, I loved our home, and envisioned all the memorable times we would have there together. It even had a small front porch, so I really saw Ryan and I raising our children there and growing old on a porch swing together.

The decorations and look of the home is what hit my borderline personality disorder the hardest, at this time. One day I would see the house one way and be outraged that we had gotten such a horrible deal, and then return any new decorative items I had purchased. Literally sometimes the very next day I would wonder why I even thought anything was wrong with the house because it was our perfectly beautiful home. I blamed it on my being overwhelmed but since it was how I had always felt, deep down I knew it was much more. Consider rose-colored glasses for a moment; one view when you look through them, and another view without them. It felt like one day I would see one vision of the house and love it, and the other day I would see a completely different vision of the house and hate it. The borderline personality disorder in me never realized that it was the same house. I would really believe that Ryan wanted the garage to stay painted red, and be so angry that he wouldn't change it. In my mind, I knew he wanted it to be red and I resented his refusal to change it. It was a stupid garage, first of all. Secondly, it was red when we purchased the home and I don't think he would've even cared what color it was. He never voiced an opinion. The other, what I call realistic feel of my borderline personality disorder is the logical side of me that knew that the only reason he didn't change the color was because he didn't care what color it was and because he was lazy.

Again, I must reiterate what a difference a few years make! In the short time that we lived there my family gave us furniture and new appliances because they knew our budget was extremely limited. We were thrilled to get new carpet and a comfy couch. We loved our new hand-me-down coffee table and matching tv unit. We just loved having our own home and family. We had fun decorating and landscaping. It was ours! We had finally made it! No matter though, my damn roller coasters just wouldn't stop! I had thought that once I got my big priorities (college, marriage, job, house purchase, etc.) out of the way, I would feel happy. I was a graduate with three degrees, had a full time job, loved my children, and finally owned a home. What the hell is wrong with me that I'm still not happy I wondered? Nothing made me happy for long though, no matter how much I accomplished or no matter what I did, it seemed. Mania would make me happy, but I still didn't know exactly what it was, except that it was a few days or weeks of the highest and most intense happiness. One day I would just feel great and attribute it to some small reason, even though I really didn't know why I felt so happy and energized. I just went with it for however long it lasted.

Ryan and I were both working, early in both of our careers, but happy with our jobs and earning potential. We fantasized about when our kids would be in college. We talked about the type of people we hoped they would become and the type of people we hoped they would eventually marry. We talked hypothetically how we would raise them during their dreaded teen years. I bragged about Taylor's preschool work, and used it as the mommy indicator that he would be brilliant because he had colored in the lines or drawn a good circle. We idealized about what we wanted for our children because it was easier than talking about how much we had failed ourselves and each other. It seemed like we could only talk about insignificant things like the weather or basic calendar plans. Anytime I asked questions, he was "always too tired, it wasn't the right time," or "I don't want to talk about it."

Ryan and I tried, but we both had our battles to beat. I needed to admit to, seek treatment for, and help myself begin recovery with my mental illnesses. I figured my strategies were enough, but that was only taking the easy way out. I also have a high spirited, demanding attitude, so I wasn't always easy to rationalize with. My grandma used to say that I could argue paint off a wall! I was adamant that I could keep it together without any help. Ryan had his own battles as well. The worst, by far, was his drinking. More often than not, this always led to abuse. My life was a constant cycle. Happy. Sad. High. Low. Healthy. Abused. The only constant in my life was the constant mood and personality swings and ever-increasing anxiety about *everything*!

I began to feel frustrated! I finally had it all, and was still unhappy. I just wondered why I couldn't ever just stop, hang on to what I had, and enjoy the moment. I had it all (I thought), but I lost it all, too. I had the perfect wedding ceremony, but a miserable marriage. I had a personable husband, but he scared the shit out of all of us with his drunken outrages. I had three college degrees, but barely was making enough to take care of the children and myself. I had a home, but was losing it because I was getting divorced and couldn't afford it alone. In other words, I did have it all. I also lost it all, so one of the hardest things I've ever had to do was try to hang on knowing that I had nothing and felt like I didn't even have hope.

Don't let go even though you've lost it all seemed to be where I had landed in nearly two years. At the time, prior to my diagnosis, that was my state of mind. I was soon-to-be divorced from Ryan, easily getting sole custody of our two children, having a hard time being both mommy and daddy, and foreclosing on a home. I was working full time, and trying to deal with an out of control lifestyle. I couldn't make ends meet each month. I was out of control because I fell apart with the knowledge that I was hopeless, and that made the bipolar in me susceptible to anything. I was scared. I would wake the kids, get them through school, take care of them every evening just like a normal parent, and then go to bed and start each day anew. The difference was that I would go days without eating anything. My son was too young to notice, so at least I had one thing to use to control my pain. Creditors were calling with threats. I was terrified of the consequences of having bad credit, and always felt anxiety over their threats. I couldn't even find the time to get by to clean the house I was hoping not to have to foreclose on because my time was already so stretched. I eased that guilt through the bipolar and borderline roller coaster, actually. When I was manic, I did a little work around the house to try to get it to sell sooner. When I was depressed, I completely took on an I don't care attitude. I was working full time and exhausted. My faith in myself was shaken. My hope of ever being happy had long since dissipated. I couldn't do it anymore. Why not let go? Now I recognize why don't let go was such an important part of my new beginning. It led me to help eventually, but it was a painful journey getting there.

At this point in my life, late twenties and early in my divorce, I was not ready to face a mental illness, so I wasn't diagnosed or medicated. I was intelligent enough to know that I was floundering though. My carefully constructed array of disguises had barely worked for twenty years, but I knew that I was on the edge of insanity and near falling off. I just couldn't cover it up anymore. I had made it through high school, college, years of a failed marriage, the adoption of my son (which was a tumultuous roller coaster in itself), and the birth of our daughter but no matter what I had made it through I just couldn't seem to make it.

I could never see the light at the end of the tunnel. Every time a new problem arose, I vehemently tackled it from every angle I knew, thinking that I could be happy once it was resolved. No matter how hard I tried something else would ultimately come up. Inner turmoil, real life problems driven too harshly by anxiety, another unexpected mental anguish, and overall problems beneath every surface layer I had.

Throughout my early adulthood, I focused solely on raising my stepdaughter, finishing college, and adopting my son, so it was easy to distract myself often enough from the problems Ryan and I had. If I could mask the problems I was having in my life and marriage, then I didn't have to deal with Ryan's uncaring nature and noticeably increasing drinking problems. Throughout high school I just pretended I was the leader of the bad crowd, but really just wanted to convince other people how powerful and invincible I was. If I could do that, no one would really notice how screwed up I was. Throughout college, since I had to commute hours daily to and from my college, I would eat only out of starvation and soon pull over for a quick purge to rid myself of all the horrible feelings that seemed glued to my insides. I had strategies to self-medicate and shadow my problems as early as a young child, and throughout my mid twenties. Could people pick up on my problems? Sure, but it was always assumed that it was due to some other circumstance or something. I spent years perfecting my disguises and fake cover-ups when it felt like the wrong personality was dominating. I made it through years of the failed marriage only because I knew that I had to stay until I *knew* there was no hope of us ever working things out. I was aware of myself enough to know that I brought a lot of problems on myself, or so it had always felt like, so I had to be certain that if I left him that it wasn't because of my mental struggles that I worked so hard to hide. As far as the pains and battles I went through to adopt my son, I may never know how

I survived that. I knew he would one day be my son, and was thrilled about that, but my moods and personalities always affected how I could interact with the biological parents that still had rights until the adoption was finalized. One day I would believe that they did try and that they did love them. No sooner that those thoughts entered my mind, I would critically think about all of the things they had cruelly done to him. It also greatly impacted my anxiety, as one day I would be thrilled and certain that I would get him, and the next day I would be convinced and terrified that the Department of Children and Families was going to take him away to give back to his biological parents. On those downhill days, as I now know that is what they are in my bipolar cycle, I would cry for hours while he was at school and be unable to sleep at night knowing I was going to lose him.

The truth of my pain began seeping out no matter how hard I tried to disguise it, so instead of fixing it I just tried to hide. I was drowning. I was depressed, quit eating nearly altogether, cried nightly in my closet after my kids were sleeping, avoided my family, attempted to avoid or ruin friendships, and kept a stash of carefully hidden razor blades…just in case. I was barely holding myself together at work. I was constantly being told that I had lost too much weight. I just attributed their words of concern as a result of me having been as big as I had been before and the difference as to how I looked now. They weren't really concerned about me, just jealous! Then my same sudden halt – hand cuffed and led to jail. Again, I fearfully told myself, don't let go. But I did. I let go. Again, and again, and again. I just couldn't keep it together, and all the previously carefully placed pieces of my puzzle crumbled and scattered wildly.

After the jail incident and criminal charges (more on that later), I realized and admitted that I needed help. That admission scared me. I confessed my own pain. That acknowledgement hurt me. I spiraled downward with friends, drugs, and men. I didn't lose control as I feared that I would. Instead, I realized that I never had control to begin with. I was at risk of losing my career and my children; in short, I was at risk of losing my heart, since my kids were the only things that kept me going. I honestly tried to live in denial and use every other strategy I could think of to cope with an illness I didn't have to face as long as I believed it wasn't true. Admitting that mental illness was true meant that I had to learn how to accept and deal with it, whatever it may be, for the rest of my life. That is also another reason why don't let go now means so much to me as a marked beginning. I just didn't know it at the time. At the time, I had no idea the hell which I would go through to hold on long enough to not let go!

I have bipolar disorder, frequently impacted by tendencies of borderline personality disorder and major mood depressive disorder, as well as generalized anxiety disorder. Sometimes I asked myself, "How screwed up can one person be? Why me? Is there a purpose? Will it always feel this much of a struggle? Be this hard?" What happened to the "let's be fair" rule we all learned in kindergarten? When you are a child, everyone has the same number of crayons in their boxes, everyone gets the same number of cookies at snack time, and everyone gets a turn to be the line leader. With my mental illnesses and problems, at the time it felt like I didn't have even a fraction of what other people had. It felt like I was always last at everything; last to do well, last to understand, last to be happy. We all know as we grow up, that life isn't fair but with a mental illness too…it just leaves me saddened and speechless, but somehow still hopeful.

Life with a mental illness is a daily battle no matter what treatment, therapy, or medication a person needs. The medication isn't a cure. Even when medications help, it may only be temporary, as medications do have to be changed due to the result of sudden and new adverse reactions. Dealing with the medications is a battle in itself. Nobody chooses mental illness, and no one can ever completely recover from the depths of it completely unscathed. Mental illness isn't a "pull yourself up by the bootstraps" situation. The hope lies within the chance that each individual suffering from a mental illness can be helped, treated, improve, recover in their own way, and become a lifelong learner and successful.

Prior to my correct diagnosis and treatment, I had lost it all though through a variety of experiences so sometimes, don't let go didn't mean anything to me! Why not let go? Did I think of suicide? Of course! Had I attempted it before? Of course! But that's not what I mean NOW when I say don't let go. What I mean is don't let go of HOPE! Unmedicated and undiagnosed, don't let go barely kept me from suicide on some days because it meant don't let go of life… yet. Don't let go barely held me through each second, minute, and hour on some days as I had all the death supplies I needed nearby. Sometimes it got the better of me, and I honestly tried suicide. Fortunately though most of the time, don't let go during these seconds, minutes, and hours helped me hang on longer, however long that may be. Correctly diagnosed and medicated, don't let go, became to mean that there was always hope.

Just as I write this, I ride the roller coaster marked by my memories of my different beginnings. The saying, "this too shall pass," comes to mind. Since receiving my list of diagnoses, if you can even call it that, and my cocktail of medications, I still have to remind myself to try to hang on and not let go sometimes. My psychiatric experiences as an adult have been miracles, but there is still only so much that medication can do. The doctors, medications, and treatments will never cure me. It is not ME that is incurable, it is the illnesses. I still ride the steep roller coaster of bipolar disorder. I still second guess everything; a small glimpse into generalized anxiety disorder. I still reach the deepest of lows in major mood depressive disorder. Likewise, I still live with the angel on one shoulder and the devil on the other shoulder, unaware of who will win every day; a very simplistic comparison to borderline personality disorder. But I CAN IMPROVE. I KNOW I CAN HANG ON FOR ONE MORE DAY, AND NOT LET GO BECAUSE THERE IS HOPE. I've already lost it all, so I might as well hang on until I know I'll never let go because I've now learned that there will always be help.

Memorable Moments

Before we go back to some of my earlier experiences, I wanted to take a moment to insert a good time memory from my youth. After all, it wasn't all about being bipolar, up or down, anxiety driven, or diverse personalities all the time. As I mentioned earlier, my memorable moments will be sporadically inserted throughout my life story just as a reminder that it wasn't all bad.

In my town, there was a special kids place where you could eat pizza, watch costume performers and even dance along with them if you wanted, play a variety of games, earn tickets to exchange for prizes, everything you can imagine to thrill a child. When I was in kindergarten one of my classmates had mentioned going to this place. I had heard of it before, but hadn't paid much attention before. I couldn't wait until I could go one day too. That afternoon when my parents picked me up, I tried to casually mention it. To my immediate surprise, we went right then and there.

For hours we danced along with the characters in their costumes, hugging them as often as I could. I had so much fun, I was practically asleep before my parents even got me out the door. We played every game at least twice, and earned what seemed like nearly a million tickets. When I stood at the counter, I could barely reach high enough to see inside, but I'm sure my eyes glowed at what I saw inside. The glass counter displayed all the contents one could trade their tickets for. Along the back wall were strung the bigger prizes that required thousands of tickets, but I didn't want any of those things anyways. I was just excited to be getting anything and thrilled about going. I have such fond memories of this experience, but I have no idea what I traded my tickets for. It didn't matter because I was happy enough being there, playing games, and being with my family. My absolute favorite thing about this place was a rotating chicken that would "cluck" an egg out if you put a token in it. The appeal was getting the prize that was inside the egg. It didn't require any skill, but was fun to play "egg roulette" to see what prize you would get. Most importantly, was the chance you had at getting the golden egg, which contained the best prize of all. The golden eggs were few, but they were beautiful. Sparkly and glossy golden. On that very first visit, I got a golden egg.

Someday

Someday I wish that I could be
happy inside, just happy with me.
Smiling outside is what on-lookers see,
while I'm fighting inside and wanting to be free.
Some think they know me through my lies and disguises
because I easily hide the sex, tears, and cries.

Age 14

CHAPTER 2

Alone And Ready For Sex

Although I have two children and am never really alone, what does it actually mean to be alone? Is it simply when we are situated by ourselves without anyone around us, or is it only when we can get our minds to quit troubling us? Bipolar alone is never really being alone, even if we are by ourselves, because the devastating inner demons of the mind never quit. If we are physically alone when we are manic, our minds are racing with the high moods that come with the mania cycle of bipolar disorder. The higher the mania, the higher the mood. Mania takes hold of your credit card and excites you about purchases you can't afford and may not even ever use. Mania takes you on spontaneous vacations that are not convenient, practical, or thought out. Mania takes you to the heights of heaven, as it is the best of everything in the world. In mania, even if individuals with bipolar are alone, their minds can't slow down enough to truly be alone. On the other hand, when in the deepest of lows of bipolar disorder, alone is still not alone. It is an uncontrollable mind game. I feel so alone. No one understands me. Why can't I just feel better? Why can't I make it go away? Should I take my own way out? Bipolar alone is the time of secrecy. It is comprised of hiding emotions, hiding suicide plans or contents, and overall just attempting to hide from yourself and the rest of the world. Bipolar alone is using your best disguises to cover your worst pains and thoughts of personal craziness, even if you're only trying to hide from yourself. It is the final admission that you can never feel any better. All of these questions and self-degrading thoughts drive the mind further into depression; so again, bipolar alone, no matter what part of the cycle, is never really alone.

Every morning I wake up, shower and dress for work, pack lunches, wake and dress two sleepy-eyed children, grab backpacks and head off to school. Routine! Routine! Routine! Something I fool myself into believing that I can control, but sometimes it's the things we convince ourselves of that get us through the day, right? Every night is the same. Pick up the kids, cook dinners, argue over eating vegetables, homework, and bedtimes…all the "normal" family stuff. Sometimes I love that time because it is precisely and preciously perfect. Safely medicated and, no other mental disorder interferences, I love those times. Safely stable as one person with an even keel mood, I enjoy laughing with my kids during dinner, splashing them in the bathtub, reading their favorite books repeatedly, and playing games outside.

Other times, bipolar lows and crashes, interferences with major mood depression, or overwhelming anxiety make me feel inadequate – leading to one of my worst enemies – guilt. The worst is the emotional crashes and the lows of bipolar and major mood depressive disorder, when I feel like crawling into my closet and crying. I feel out of body, out of place, and helplessly unhappy. The emotion may be able to hide behind the floodgates until my kids are in bed, but then sometimes I still feel like I fall to pieces. My beautiful babies are sleeping and happily dreaming, and their mommy is falling apart and crying in the closet. Hiding.

Hurting. Without the stability of my medication, I secretly and silently blame the kids for all my terrible feelings. Even though I logically know that it isn't their faults that their mommy is losing control, I honestly believe and feel like it is all their faults. I can say that I never take it out on them, but in some ways it does impact them. I have never been abusive or neglectful to them, but when I'm not as stable and too low, I'm not the mommy they are use to. We don't eat meals together, let alone laugh. We don't play games inside or outside. Instead we lazily watch countless hours of t.v. As far as reading to them goes, I don't even try when I'm that low. I wonder if anyone has any idea how hard it is to look in the eyes of a begging two year old and say no when she is asking to sit in your lap and read to her? It's not hard at all when your so low that you don't think you'll even live long enough for her to even remember you. Such extremes! My life has always revolved around such extremes!

Stable or unstable though, at least I'm still somehow always hoping. That is one of the miracles of the right treatment plan. I may fall apart, but at least it doesn't leave the razor-sliced visible bloodlines and scars on my wrist like it did in the past unmedicated. It may leave me with tear stained-cheeks sometimes, but at least I'm alive to be able to cry!

Hope for individuals with bipolar disorder or borderline personalities is sometimes a different kind of hope, though, just as the meaning of alone is different for individuals with bipolar. It is, and most likely always will be, a varied hope. I hope I can make it comfortably through the day. I hope I can be at ease with myself tomorrow. I hope I don't crash soon. Then the inevitable, another crash, which only brings about the lows of hope. I hope I accidentally die in a car accident today. I hope someone offers to pick up the kids so that I don't have to deal with them today and I have more time to cry. I hope I get physically ill enough from a cold that I'm able to stay in bed and avoid the world for a week. I hope that no one notices that I'm silently screaming because I feel that frantic parts of me falling apart. I hope no one notices the perfectly selected jewelry and clothes are only to disguise my pain and suffering. I just hope there is a means to an end.

Fortunately for me, the emotional lows and crashes aren't as frequent or always as long lasting as I know they are for other people. My mania, however, is enough to almost make me want to quit taking the medications altogether because it feels so good except I remember the hell I barely survived without them. With this in mind, some bipolar patients do actually opt out of medication because they enjoy the mania so much. How they handle the lows, I'll never be able to understand, but we all have our different strengths and weaknesses. My mania is a beautiful thing, as it marks the beginning of the roller coaster ascending again and leading me back up and out of the darkness.

When I'm manic, I feel beautiful, sexy, overconfident, and able to conquer the world…or at least the world of men. Although this is not always necessarily true, bipolars and borderlines often switch into this role. Since my highest scaled disorder is bipolar, I attribute it to that, but the borderline personality tendencies also help remind me how perfect I am when I'm manic. When I'm manic, every raindrop to my skin feels like a satin touch. In mania, the wind blowing though my hair gives me chills. In the summer downpours of rain, mania makes me want to twirl around in circles getting soaked until my hair is wet and streaked down to my face. Mania makes me want to feel the music when I'm driving, as opposed to only hearing it. The thump of the bass feels like my heart thumps with feeling along with the music. Mania is a super sensory feeling when everything just feels blissfully electrifying.

Embarrassingly enough, my roadmap and structure that expressed my high when I was manic was sex. Sex drove me further into mania, and who wouldn't love feeling that happy? I didn't always know what made me go so low or go so manic. Maybe I never will know. What I do know though, is that sex was my self-medication that reinforced the mania when my roller coaster went just beyond the edges of too high. Coming out of the lows, I feel better. Ascending into mania, I feel the need of control and power. Once near or in mania, I was determined for sex as it was my drug, my addiction, my highest of highs. It was like an unstoppable progression that I couldn't stop. As soon as I'd start to notice the first signs of mania, I knew I was going to feel out of control and sex crazed before it was all over. As cool as that may sound to someone who does not struggle with mental illnesses, or even to people with mental illness, it was also as frustrating as satisfying. Considering I couldn't exactly have sex whenever and wherever I want to, it could also aggravate my mania too. No matter how you look at it, being manic had just as many pitfalls as the low end of bipolar does.

The problem was the obvious. I had a professional career, was responsible, tried my best to lovingly raise two children, worked full time, and lived as healthily and safely as I could. I would never let my high drive for sex interfere with the lives of my children, but when I was in mania, behind closed doors I practically took every opportunity that I could. Not that it made me a whore. I never said it lowered my expectations, but the cravings for sex were always at its strongest during mania. Why? Because of the sensory stimulation, I assume. Because of the powerful feeling of making another person feel good. Because, figuratively speaking, when you're at the top of the world, why not reach a little higher? It didn't matter if it was a fling with a long time friend, a one nighter with someone else, or a longer lasting relationship, I thrived on the sensations of sex when I was manic. You already feel good, so why not go for feeling the best ever? Although it hardly ever ended that way.

On several occasions, I can think of a "fling" that probably shouldn't have happened for one reason or another, but mania takes a life of its own and the draw to sex becomes magnetic. A few times with a college student nearly ten years younger than me. A few times with a man I knew was wrong for me. A few times with an ex who was phone call away, a for one reason only friend. It didn't matter, as long as I was manic, all I wanted was the good feelings, both mental and physical, from manic sex. I didn't need to hear I love you, any level of commitment, or even true feelings. I just needed the sexual satisfaction that matched the high and exaggerated physical and intellectual satisfaction I already felt in mania.

Memorable Moments

Regardless of mental illnesses, physical illnesses, and setbacks, we can always treasure the memorable moments because they help us to not let go!

The first time I went to the skating rink was with my mom. It was just the two of us. I was so young that my brother hadn't even been born yet. The local roller skating rink was divided into two skating sections; one rink where skaters gracefully and skillfully circled around the rink, and the back practice room for new learners like myself. Practically the whole time we were there we spent in that room. I didn't mind though. I was just excited that I was doing something so "big girl" with my mom. I looked up to her. She was strong enough to help me off the floor the numerous times I fell, brave enough to try to help me, and loving enough to kiss my knees when I fell and laughingly tried to climb back up. She was my rock.

The irony of this good time is that it is significant in more way than one. It was one of my fondest of memories of just the two of us because it was fun. I fell, she fell, we fell. We stumbled back up and did it all over again. My mom was the first person to actually get me all the way around "the big kids rink". The one time she risked leading me out of the practice room was only because I begged and insisted that I had to make it around the "big kids rink" just once. Because of her, we did. She saved me from falling and getting hurt.

She continued to do that in other ways for years, and in many ways still does. Who would've ever thought that a first trip to the skating rink would have such a strong correlation to life that many years later. The few pictures my mom and I took of each other when we were there was when either of us was on our butt, which was most of the time!

Just Stop It All

Each breath I try a little more
to just forget the pain.
But every try is useless now
and my attempts are in vain.
With every beating of my heart
I cry a little more.
I wish there was another way out
but death is at my door.
With every whisper from my mouth
I heave a fearful dread.
I feel I'm losing all my pieces
and my world is already feeling dead.
My eyelids growing heavy now
and all I see is black.
My thoughts are fading rapidly
and hope is what I lack.

Age 13

CHAPTER 3

Dating, Loving, And . . . Escaping

Prior to my treatment, as I mentioned, my marriage had rapidly crumbled and was near ending bitterly in divorce. I will take my fair share of the blame, as I was obviously unmedicated, and obviously needed to be. I do not believe we could've survived our marriage anyways, but I will never completely know since I wasn't diagnosed or medicated until after the divorce. Maybe I was the one to blame. Maybe my illnesses impacted me more than his addictions. I had faithfully dated and been married to Ryan for ten years. I have only been married once, to Ryan, my first true love. Right or wrong for me, I threw caution to the winds. My insides were screaming, "NO," but I was twenty-two, wanted all my dreams to come true, and thought I was ready to help him and myself. I thought we could help each other in the process of beginning a household and family. I wanted to be with him. He made me feel special. We were in love since early in our relationship, and within months, were living together. We had many great years, but as my illnesses continued to thrive strongly within my own mind, his physical addictions also ravaged away at him.

Our dating was rather uneventful, other than that gut wrenching feeling that something isn't right that I had on occasion. Not that he was specifically to blame, but I just had a wrong feeling from time to time. We had a glorious time, but I also had concerns too. We would go on dates, be as sexually mischievous as several other couples are early in relationships, spend friendly evenings with each other's families, spend holidays and times off from work and college together. We just seemed to have the best of both worlds, but that was normal for me so I didn't see it as any different. I had always experienced the highest of highs and the lowest of lows. I had always experienced one person driving my life and then seemingly like an entirely different person running it at other times. My dating relationship with Ryan is comparable because we had plenty of both good and horrible times.

Ryan came from a long line of "social drinkers" (or so they thought) but it would leave me with the wrong feeling on more than one occasion. He also had a wandering eye, and a job that allowed secrecy. I was trusting because I wanted to be. I was burned by my trust because I didn't use my common sense and good judgment. My borderline disorder tendencies caused a huge bother to the relationship. Regardless of whether or not Ryan was being unfaithful or not, I would either be head over heels in love with him full well knowing that he wasn't, or I wouldn't speak to him for days because I was convinced he was. I would lecture him about doing the laundry a certain way that wasn't the way I thought it should be done. Even simplistic things, my bipolar disorder allowed me to make into even bigger issues.

We flew for frequent vacations anywhere that we wanted to go. We went skiing. We toured Vanderbilt and some of the finest wineries, museums, and tourist highlights in many states. We learned the history of states such as Florida by visiting St.

Augustine and sketching the horse drawn carriages and terraced buildings. We went to New York City to pay our respects after September 11th and, on several other occasions for Broadway shows. We cruised to Mexico, Jamaica, and Grand Cayman. We were young and in love, and pretended to be carefree. It was fun, and the lack of grown up responsibility sometimes was too tantalizing. Unfortunately even these times were impacted by my mental illnesses. If the flights were even one second late it sent me into an emotional upheaval. If our luggage didn't arrive as expected, I imagined the worst or just suggested that we didn't need any of it for the vacation anyways. I wasn't afraid of flying, but anything having to do with airports put me in a bipolar low because it was too much negative stimulation. Ryan was used to the airport chaos though, but never truly recognized how much I was bothered by it. Then again, he didn't know or recognize that I had several mental illnesses.

We lived carefree, but I didn't feel carefree. Again, this was prior to my diagnosis and treatment, but my mind just felt that things weren't right. How much of this was because of me though, I wondered? I had always known that I was different, confirmed by earlier inpatient stays, so was it just my issues that were haunting me yet again? I knew I felt uneasy. Did I feel uneasy because my emotions and personalities were often all over the place, and I feared he would someday figure it out? Was I hesitant because he drank more than I was comfortable with, more than most people, and was more aggressive than most people were after drinking? I just didn't know how much of it was him and how much of it was me, so I didn't let go. Still, his daughter, Noel, was loved tremendously by both of us, but my heart knew even then that I was her protector.

Two weeks before my marriage, I wandered into the kitchen and noticed the jerky nervous movements of my soon-to-be husband as he rushed to get off the Internet. I was shocked at his embarrassed surprise when I walked in the room. Never in a million years did I expect it to be the life-altering answers I received after I asked a few questions. With my soon-to-be stepdaughter happily watching t.v. in the next room, I casually asked what he was doing. "Just checking my email," he replied. "Why were you being so secretive? Were you trying to hide something?" I began to pry. The look on his face gave it away; he was hiding, and I couldn't let go until I knew. He said that he had been Instant Messaging a friend after checking his email and was embarrassed about the conversation. Since the friend Ryan was referring to was gay, the most logical question I could think to ask next was, "are you gay?" At that point, we were walking outside because I knew that the truth was going to knock the wind out of me and I didn't want his daughter to witness that. I nervously fingered the ring on my ring finger, and the puffiness of the scar underneath it from a twenty year old injury.

He leaned up against the side of the house, nonchalantly, as if discussing the music that would be played in the background of our reception during the meal. He wasn't scared. He was confident. He didn't appear nervous, so I expected a response that would piss me off, but not damage me to the magnitude that it did. "I've been cheating on you," he admitted, "and I really care about her." I chocked back words. I gulped for breath. Too many scenarios ran through my head. I lost any words I could muster. Worse yet, I lost trust, love, communication, and our connection. It was two weeks before my very expensive wedding, and I was finding out that the love of my life had been unfaithful on more than one occasion. I felt the anger rising. I was at the boiling point where the steam rises, but there is no way for it to escape. All I could do was punch him. Common sense, dignity, self control, deferring right from wrong…all of it was gone, and the only thing left to ease my pain was to cause pain to the one who hurt me the most. The one who I was supposed to vow to love forever in a matter of days, who had just shattered my heart into a million pieces. That was obviously a huge part of the problem, but it was also a huge trigger that immediately sent me into a bipolar frenzy! I couldn't slow down. My mind raced.

I hurt. I was angry. I was scared. I was high from the mania of all the wedding activities that had been going on, but my roller coaster dropped as I learned of his unfaithfulness. Again, I let go.

Two weeks later, as planned, we were married. Broken hearted or not, I just didn't know how to handle it all in the time that I felt that I had. I really did love him, and Noel practically owned half my heart. I figured we could somehow make it work still. Our wedding was an absolute beautiful dream wedding. We had everything a princess bride would want, and I gloated in the attention of the beauty of me, the church, pictures, decorations, reception hall, etc. For that night, I was a princess. I floated on the dance floor, I glided around hugging with teary eyed guests, I giggled with my girlhood best friends, and I dreamily thought of the life I knew would evolve into what everyone else thought I already had. Would I have decided not to marry him if I had found out earlier? Still to this day, I do not know. Even more significant and important though, my son, Taylor, was born the same week. Although at the time he was only my nephew on Ryan's side of the family, before he was four we had legally adopted him.

I made the first call to the Department of Children and Families to report the suspected abuse of my nephew, and his two siblings. I knew was that this little boy was meant for me as much as I was meant for him. I could feel how much we needed each other. I spent the next few years meeting with caseworkers, attorneys, and group meetings with caseworker managers. I spent my nights following his biological parents so that I could report their wrongdoings to the caseworker. They were perfect manipulators, so the only way to prove their abuse and neglect was to outsmart the expert con artists. Many nights I would hide discreetly in the parking lot of their favorite bars, see them drive in, call their social worker, and then wait for her to report back to me the next day.

If there had been any doubt in my mind that his parents were capable I wouldn't have encouraged the system so strongly, but the need was obvious. Through all this fight, I convinced myself that my husband was equally involved, supportive, and driven. Little did I know that he was hiding the liquor bottles in his trunk and drinking every time he had a chance (mostly while driving!). I was swearing to the social worker that we had a beautiful family that was ready to provide Taylor with a loving home, completely unaware of what was really going horribly wrong on in my own home.

Sure, we had our problems, but I really believed that we were a wonderful family with a good home. It wasn't until we were well on the way and near the end of the road for the adoption that I started really discovering the magnitude of his/our problems. So what that my husband violated me by stripping me and taking un-consented naked pictures of me when I was sleeping? So what that I had to run away with Noel from time to time until he passed out so that she wasn't harmed by Ryan's drunken outbursts? After all, I knew Ryan was sorry and he promised change. It couldn't have happened that frequently, could it? So what if he was more drawn to secrecy? He was entitled to his own privacy, right?

I fought to adopt my son. I fought for Taylor because he didn't have anyone else, and I fought hard. All along I had been the voice for Ryan and I, so it was not new to me that I be the speaker for this situation. I honestly believed that our problems were fixable and mentioned them to one of the many caseworkers we had. She agreed that we were on the right track and to keep up the progress. If only I had known how much the adoption process impacted my moods! Again, my bipolar went through many cycles of highs and lows. My emotions rode the steep ride along with every little bump, turn, and curve of the process, when realistically it was practically impossible that his biological parents could get him back and no one else wanted him. Nonetheless I was constantly extraordinarily high fully knowing that I would get him, or I was deep in the depths of hell with fear that I would lose him. Granted it wasn't all final until it was final, but I know my moods were extreme as a result of how extreme I took any piece of news or information from the Department of Children and Families system.

Truth be told, I stayed in a bad marriage longer than I should have. I had lost hope, but I did want us to work out. Consider the difference between hope, want, and need. I stayed until he had another job and enrolled into a drug and alcohol program. I stayed until he proved that he wasn't even willing to decrease the drama of his alcoholism. I stayed until I knew Noel was old enough to choose to stay with her mother and be safe without me. I stayed until I hated him for hurting my children, and not loving anyone of us enough to be faithful, truthful, and at least attempt recovery. I didn't expect him to do it perfectly, otherwise I would've left him when it all started. I did expect to at least see him try though, and if anything, it was obvious that he was making it worse than ever before.

Would I have still adopted Taylor if I had known that I would be divorcing my Ryan, raising Taylor on my own, and not giving him the family life the courts prefer? A million times over, YES! Of course it saddens me that I can't give Taylor everything I dreamed that I could, but his life is precious and highly enjoyed. I can't blame Ryan for everything that went wrong in our marriage, but I wouldn't have ever thought twice about adopting Taylor. I always knew that I would adopt Taylor if I could, even with the depth and extensiveness of his problems. When it comes to the marriage, again I reiterate that it takes two to make or break love, but I have wondered who won the title of the most blame? Me, for being who I am and who I was, or him for continuing to be who he was and denying there was ever a problem. He could cure himself of his problems, if he ever put his mind to it. I couldn't. When it comes to blame in a divorce, it doesn't really matter. The biggest surprise came to me much later when Ryan's carelessly and obviously negative behavior worsened. Ryan had always been good at hiding though, so most of the time I spent anxiously and suspiciously watching him.

Ryan and I had our huge differences, but I hadn't completely given up yet otherwise one of us would've already filed for divorce. We had major issues, but I had to continue my daily living to the best that I could until I could figure out how to fix the problems. Since it was the winter season, I had picked up a cold and just couldn't seem to kick it. Congestion, runny nose, sore throat, everything just hurt! I missed a few days of work, so I figured I might as well go to the Doctor and get an antibiotic. After grimacing over my weight (since I was at a heavy phase again), I was led back to a room. The nurse came in and did her typical routine procedures and asked all the normal questions. Since I have always had an abnormal menstrual cycle (most likely due to the years of anorexia) it was common-place for me to take a pregnancy test before they would give me any medications. Just in case. Every time I always felt pretty certain that I wasn't pregnant since the marriage hadn't been so great and we weren't exactly in the mood very often, but I always did it since it was part of their normal protocol with me. After awkwardly peeing on a stick for what seemed like the hundredth time, since this was typical treatment for me at a clinic I had been going to for a while, I returned to my room to wait for the Doctor. It seemed like hours before the Doctor came in. I was sick, so I just figured that the wait felt longer than it really was because I was feeling lousy. A nurse finally checked in with me, so I jokingly said, "well, I guess I'm not pregnant, huh?" She comfortably replied, "I just wanted to let you know that the Doctor will be just another minute or so," and she apologized that it had taken so long. I still had no idea. The thought that I might be pregnant never crossed my mind.

The Doctor came in, asked how I was feeling, asked about my symptoms, and apologized for being late. It was a normal Doctor and patient conversation. The next thing I knew, all the nurses and Doctors at the clinic came busting into the room with flowers squealing, "congratulations, you ARE pregnant!" Immediately I was consumed with joy. Planned or not, I was more excited (and surprised) than I had ever been in my entire life. The Doctors had obviously assumed that I had always wanted to get pregnant since I was married, but that I had just obviously had a difficult time due to the irregular cycles. They even excitedly told me that they loved telling patients who really wanted to be pregnant, as opposed to women they knew definitely didn't want to be pregnant. The nurses said that they even did the test twice since the color of the line on the pee stick was so light. She reasoned that it was because I had so recently become pregnant that it was barely showing yet. It wasn't that I didn't want to get pregnant, but I already knew the marriage was beyond repair, so the timing wasn't exactly perfect. Nonetheless, I immediately started thinking about all the wonderful things about pregnancy, having a baby, raising a baby, and dreaming about the wonderful connection I knew I would have with my daughter. I already had the perfect son, so I just knew this baby would be my perfect daughter.

I cannot speak for Ryan; therefore, I cannot directly say whether or not he wanted the baby. As the years have gone by since we adopted Taylor, I have also questioned whether or not Ryan even wanted him. Of course my perceptions could be completely wrong, I'll admit to that, but there has always been a difference in his relating to his biological children than his adopted child. However his interactions with them are very infrequent, so I do not necessarily have many times to compare to. Nonetheless, I'll hope for the best in him, and say that he did want our children. I'll hope that he felt the joy, amazement, and wonder that I did with both of our wonderful children. After such a surprise with our daughter (which I admittedly considered scary and exciting) Ryan's only response was "Oh shit! Oh shit! Oh shit!" Of course I was scared because, by this time, I already felt divorce was probable and beyond just possible. I was still tremendously excited about having a baby and open-minded enough to see if things could work though. My gut feelings were that we couldn't overcome the magnitude of our problems together because it felt like I was closer to reaching out for help than he was, but I was still willing to wait and see. He just seemed so nonchalant about the baby regardless of the status of our marriage. He never looked for a way out of it, but he didn't have to because I left him when she was only a few months old. I wish he could've been healthier, and had a better relationship with his children, but there is always hope for recovery and a New Beginning. Maybe he just isn't ready for his. I do not hope for his recovery for the purpose of reconciling our marriage, but from the perspective that I would love for my children to have an honest, attempting recovery, and safe daddy.

I hadn't been diagnosed yet, but I wouldn't have been able to take my medications anyways even if I had been. Several medications used to treat bipolar disorder are not safe to take while pregnant. My doctor did prescribe one of the safe antidepressants for me though since depression was what I had previously been treated for by the general practitioner for a quite a while. In reference to how being bipolar impacted my pregnancy though it never seemed to impact my emotions toward the baby. That was about the only thing it didn't impact though. As I mentioned before several times, I was increasingly becoming more and more mentally unstable, so in that single regard, the pregnancy wasn't any easier than any of the other emotional episodes I had. I would be angry about work, and then boast about how I was the best at the job. I would dislike one person one day, and act as if we were friends the next day because that was how I honestly felt. I would envision Ryan and I raising our children as a loving couple, then be outraged at him when he came home drunk and angry within the week even though I knew to expect that from him. My emotional roller coaster was as bad as it had always been, but for the first time ever, it was lessened because I had the best two things in the world to look forward to: the finalization of the adoption, and the birth of my daughter.

Practically until the day the baby was born, I happily shopped for baby clothes, furniture, accessories…everything I thought I would need. Little did I know as a first time mother to a newborn, all you really need is a lot of diapers, bottles, and opportunities to sleep. Nonetheless, I had the easiest and most beautiful experience with my pregnancy. I hardly even had morning sickness, loved her specific cravings, hoped the memories of how it felt when she hiccupped inside me would never fade, loved going to the Doctor, loved seeing her squirm on the ultrasounds...I just treasured and loved every minute. I loved the attention I got from everyone about how cute pregnant mothers always looked. I loved the questions about her and my pregnancy. I loved the connection I felt with her. Ryan couldn't even remember her due date or how many weeks along I was and was more repulsed by the way I looked, as opposed to the comforting things others would say about my appearance. Don't get me wrong, I know pregnant women aren't exactly tiny but Ryan's lack of interest, understanding, and support felt like a direct hit at our family and newly coming baby. Not to mention, it crushed my already damaged self esteem. I can honestly say that we only "made love" once throughout my entire pregnancy because it was so lackluster of love and he was so careless and uncaring that it hurt. I was all the more willing, don't get me wrong, but it felt like a violation because I could tell it was only for him. No kissing, no foreplay, no love, so much so that he didn't even bother trying after that. My heart broke and I wanted out, but at the same time, I was terrified about raising two children on my own, especially considering one of them would be a baby. What did I know about taking care of children when I couldn't even manage to take care of myself or Ryan?

Taylor was more active in Anna's pregnancy that Ryan was, in his own young and heart felt way. Taylor loved putting his small hand on his mommy's belly and feeling his baby sister kicking or moving. He thought it was the coolest thing. I remember he even wanted to take me to show and tell one week at preschool so his friends could feel my belly. Needless to say I didn't exactly go for that, but Taylor was adorably cute about the pregnancy and his excitement about having a baby sister soon. He also loved thumbing through the few scrapbook pages of her ultrasound pictures, and watching her ultrasound video. He just laughed and laughed about how much she was flipping around in the video. He was protective of her, always asking if I was doing things that were okay for her too. For example, he wasn't sure I was allowed to eat birthday cake since it had sugar so I got a lecture before I even got a slice of my own birthday cake! Again though, I loved his caring and sensitivity. He began to resent his daddy during this time even more so though, because he took some of Ryan's actions, especially his drinking and anger, as an offense towards not only him (and his self esteem), but to his unborn sister too. Taylor also loved listening to her heartbeats with an at home monitor. I would laugh as we rubbed the jelly over my enormous belly, and he would carefully move the sensor around until he could hear her heartbeat. He always talked about how her heart was beating fast because she was happy, or she wouldn't stay still for him to hear her heartbeat because she was excited. He liked trying to talk to her. He played his favorite songs for her. He loved his sister before he even knew her. Everything he had to say about her was always endearingly cute. He was already the perfect big brother before she was even born.

Ryan went off the charts in a total opposite direction. He drank all the time, and I was constantly having to shuffle Taylor and Noel to their grandparents so that they were safe. At first Ryan would come home almost appearing normal. I could never go by smell or breath though because he knew I would pay close attention to it in case it was an indicator. He always had a supply of breath mints. Then he would begin stumbling around more, acting more aggressive, argumentative, and frustrated than usual. This would lead to my inevitable question, "have you been drinking?" He always said no, and had a million reasons why it was just me being crazy, but it was always only a matter of time before I would be in the position to get hurt. Ryan threw plates and dishes, smashed lamps, kicked anything in his path.

He screamed. He cursed. He walked aimlessly around our yard screaming about the kids and I. It was always a scene. Before it ever got this bad I always had Taylor and Noel safely at their grandmothers, and I left him so soon after Anna was born that she wasn't exposed to it. It was always the same with Ryan though. Almost like a list of steps to put something together; he'd come home from somewhere, try to avoid me for just a little while, start trying to mask his drunkenness by acting silly, get aggravated or angry, start shouting, and then I'd know it was my cue to escape with the kids. Once I had them safely at their grandmother's house, I would dumbly always go back to try to calm him down or clean up his mess so that the kids didn't even have to see it. If he was there and awake when I got back, the smashing, throwing, and exploding would resume. If he was gone, I knew he had gone out to drink for the night, and that I'd have plenty of time to clean up. He always went through the same steps before nearly hurting me, and causing me to leave my own home until he passed out and it was safe to go back. It was the pieces of his puzzle and they fit together, but it wasn't a safe fit for the kids or myself.

He skipped doctor appointments with me that were about the baby, and even left me once at one all alone because he was already drunk and in a rage. He made excuses not to go with me to the birthing classes, only for me to come home and find him drunk. His anger was evident. I just didn't know the cause, but I knew he was angry no matter if he was drunk or not. He was always mad about something. Honestly, I don't think I cared about the cause of his anger anymore. I was a mother hen and when feeling threatened, a mother hen protects her chicks. I didn't try to protect him from himself and I wasn't concerned at all with protecting our marriage anymore. At that point, I just started making plans and considering ideas for how to escape from it all. I already felt guilty for putting Taylor in the position to endure more suffering similar to what he had already endured for years before I was able to get him, and I couldn't imagine raising a baby in a house that could damage the souls and bodies of all of us.

The closer we came to Anna's birth the heavier I felt and the more ready I was to be able to get out of bed instead of roll out of bed. The last few Doctors appointments were pretty physically uncomfortable too, but Ryan didn't make it to a single one. The closer we got to her due date, the less she appeared to want to meet the world. My doctor and I decided together the day my daughter would be born. We planned to induce labor on a particular date, so we essentially picked her birth date. What should've been a husband and wife decision, if ever possible, was a decision that I made with my doctor because Ryan was too busy, drunk, or angry to come. I missed Ryan so much. Even if he and I weren't working out well, I had always dreamed of the perfect pregnancy scenario, and it would've been nice if I could've shared more of those moments with him. Planning for her birth date was needless though because she was actually born on her due date. I had a slow labor at home for two days, alternating between taking warm baths and showers and trying to stay comfortable in bed. To be honest, it just hurt too much to walk, like they always suggest. Ryan had planned to take time off from work, so he was off for a few weeks but I didn't see much of him, especially when I was laboring. I'm sure it's not easy to just stand by and watch someone hurting and feel helpless, but I would've loved to be comforted by him being next to me, timing contractions, encouraging me, getting me small drinks (since we had a two story house that didn't make it easy to get to and from the kitchen in labor), or acting the least bit excited. I don't even know where he spent his time off before our baby was born. I know he didn't spend much of the daytime or early night hours at home though. We were still sleeping in the same bed, so it wasn't as if our relationship had reached the definite stage of divorce, but I missed him and was also angry at him at the same time that he didn't seem to care about communicating.

Finally the big day came! My beautiful baby girl Anna was

born, my miracle came to greet the world! I had labored at home for two days while Ryan slept, drank, and abused drugs. Granted I was manic knowing that she would be born soon so even though I could barely get out of bed, I couldn't sleep either because I felt so wired. At this point I didn't care about the stupid decisions Ryan made, I was just excited and ready to meet my angelic baby. I decided to go to the hospital in the early morning hours around four a.m. I had called Ryan's mother to come and stay with Taylor and take him to school and back to her house later in the day. Timing contractions before it was time to leave was actually almost fun. Don't get me wrong it hurt like hell, but it also just made me realize that I was that much closer to her birth, which I was very excited about. Ryan slept through the contractions and timing that night, but maybe that is what all men do. I wouldn't know. He even wanted to stop at a convenience store on the way to the hospital at four a.m. so that he could buy cigarettes. Needless to say, that conversation didn't even progress into an argument as I was pretty far into labor and had no problem making my demands! Absolutely not! Ryan even slept in the delivery room on and off almost all the way up to just moments before Anna was born (early in the afternoon, by the way) while my mom and dad supported and coached me through her birth. Regardless of the circumstances, history, or any other factor, the day I adopted Taylor and shook the Judge's hand, and the day I felt my Anna's head as she was being delivered just moments before I held her were the most special moments of my life. I will never forget the warmth that filled my heart. My earth moved. All pain or suffering vanished immediately.

As soon as the nurses took Anna to clean her and prepare her to give back to me, I felt like I missed her already. Just as people claimed I would feel, I instantly fell in love with her and didn't want to be away from her for even a moment. All I wanted in my life anymore was my children. They were now the most important things to me in the entire world, and I knew that meant making some changes when we returned home. It was hard enough having to be away from Taylor, but at least I knew he was safe at his grandmothers. Moments later they brought Anna back. I had her room in with me, so the only times she was away from me was when she had her routine check ups along with all the other babies. The evening of the afternoon that she was born, they came to get her for her first bath. I happily went with her, and helped to give her her first bath. Ryan wasn't even there, but I was beyond caring about what he did. I'll admit that my anger and frustration at him may very well be due to my mental illnesses, but nonetheless, I wanted and needed him (or so I thought) so I was disappointed and even more protective of my children as a result. He seemed too far removed already.

Ryan and I were fighting before we left the hospital. I would not let my baby princess out of my hands for a second. Already he was being too loud, leaving us in the hospital to drunkenly go out, and seemingly uninterested in Anna. We weren't even out of the hospital yet, and already his inner demons were tormenting us. Wonder of all wonders, Ryan ran into a friend whose wife was also giving birth while we were at the hospital. Ryan and his friend left several times throughout the next few days to celebrate Anna's birth by driving around, drinking, and smoking pot. He was with me when she was born, however out of it he may have been, and he stuck around some after she was born. Unfortunately those days for him are probably blurred because he spent a lot of that time drinking and doing drugs with his friend. I was too in love with my daughter to care though. I knew the wife of Ryan's friend, but since she was as busy with her new family edition as I was, I never did get the chance to see her. I hope her baby's father grew up more than mine did. Even if Ryan loves his children more than anything, sometimes love isn't enough. So here I was leaving the hospital knowing that my love for Ryan wouldn't be enough.

Ryan hadn't changed at all. Of course, with my bipolar still running rampant, I went through the unmedicated roller coaster that goes along with it. I just couldn't escape the damn roller coaster of highs and lows no matter how hard I tried. Regardless I was beginning to realize that there was no hope for us, but I'll admit that any kind of help with a newborn from her daddy would've been nice. On the way to taking Taylor to a children's party, Ryan decided to get a few beers. Since the baby was less than a month old, I had stayed home with her since it was an evening party. It was actually a celebration party at the preschool where Taylor attended. By the time Ryan reached the scene of the party, he was already drunk, and crashed his car into the ditch. "Don't tell your mommy," he told Taylor. For years too, Taylor was too afraid to tell me "because he was afraid his daddy would get mad at him." The sad part is that, again, it was passed by and Taylor could've fallen through the cracks by others who were in a position to help him. Surely the people who worked at the preschool knew the difference in Ryan's behaviors, but none of them stopped him from allowing Taylor to get back in the car and ride home with him after the party was over.

A week later Ryan had been out, supposedly working, while I was home with the Taylor and Anna. He was going to pick up Noel and her best friend up from the movies after he got off work and bring them home for a spend the night at our house. By the time Ryan got home with the girls, I was so embarrassed and scared for them because it was obvious that he was past the point of being drunk. Ryan was drunk and pissed! He threw the contents of our house in the yard. He yelled and screamed at me in the middle of our front yard. A couple walking by asked if things were ok, and he swaggered towards them and said we were fine. Taylor was watching Blues Clues in his room, Noel was in her room with her best friend watching a movie, newborn Anna was sleeping in her bassinet, and I was nervously trying to hold it together and just get Ryan to pass the hell out so that none of us had to deal with him. To add insult to injury, that same week I could tell that when Ryan was handling the baby too roughly it was definitely because he had been drinking. I was frustrated and completely bipolar again. Over the next few days I felt angry at his actions and risks to the children that night, but I also felt manic about how much better off we were all going to be without him. I would pack some of our things planning to leave, and then remember how much I used to love him and wonder, what if…the borderline and bipolar ruled my life no matter the circumstances. Back and forth. One person then another. High and low. With no stops allowed.

Honestly, through all Ryan's array of lying and living in denial, a teeny tiny part of me still did want our marriage to work. If for no other reason, I wanted things to work due to the fact that I loved parts of our history and for the sake of our two children. My relationship with him felt like my life in general. They both felt like a love and hate relationship. Ryan and I had some terrible times, but we also had some great times. I think that is why I let the struggles go on for so long. I had terrible, horrifically awful things happen to me, but I also lived fortunately, with all the possible positive experiences right there for my taking. I don't even know if that was possible though because after years of abuse I had already fallen out of love with him. He even excitedly told me during my maternity leave that he was proud of himself because he had been able to start growing marijuana in our backyard. I was outraged, but what else was new? Most of Ryan's actions outraged me. I had started circling the days he was drinking to show him the evidence of the problem. I had his family members talk to him. His mother even paid for him to enroll in a program. Fairly said, a part of me did want a healthy relationship with him. Even though I had complete reason to be angry with him, my own roller coaster was still plaguing me so. I didn't feel any more stable within than the behaviors he exhibited. The only difference was that my inner turmoil didn't impact the kids the way his alcoholic abusive behaviors did.

Then that rainy day that, again, reminds me how hard going through my journey to finding my new beginning was. There were so many times and so many strategies that I thought would help Ryan. I tried being supportive. I tried monitoring his drinking. I tried going complete prohibition. I even started sneaking through his car and trunk and finding huge stashes of alcohol bottles. All stolen from work too (obvious by the label). I would dump them down the sink only to find them replaced a week later. I tried guilt tripping him into stopping for the sake of our marriage, our careers, our children, but nothing seemed to work. Maybe I was tackling it from the wrong direction, I'll never know. I do know that nothing I did helped him, and I hope that one day he, too, is able to conquer his own inner demons. It's possible for anyone, so it's even possible for him. The drinking wouldn't have been such a problem if he wasn't an abusive alcoholic, but he was always mean in addition to getting drunk too often, and it always led to a risk that love didn't make worth taking.

In the pouring down rain, Ryan stood in the doorway of our house and told me that he had been fired from his job because of his drinking! I was literally speechless. It had to be due to some kind of mistake that could easily be figured out, I thought, because there is no reason they would have to fire him even if he did slip up. He had been a good employee for several years. Then the story came out. The previous night he had gotten drunk and caused such a drunken scene that the Hartsfield International Airport was temporarily shut down until he could be controlled. It all started because he was in a bad mood and decided to have quite a few drinks at the bar. After becoming far beyond obliterated, he decided to walk onto the empty planes on the runway and grab a few free beers, since the liquor was usually already stocked on planes in order for them to be prepared for flight. He wandered the airport runways and ramps, going from one plane to another and taking all the liquor and beer he could find. He drank them, and then just threw the bottles aside on the tarmac. He was careless, carefree, and a danger to the safety of himself, airport staff, security, and passengers. Needless to say, the airport security didn't exactly take that incident too lightly.

The next morning his employer tested him for drugs and alcohol, and failed. Immediately he was put on unpaid leave until his termination papers could be delivered. Nearly ten years in a great career, and he gave it all up and lost it because he wasn't willing to seek recovery. Fired because of the same habits that were tearing us apart. I did give it one last honest shot though. When Ryan enrolled into an A.A. program and the program that his mother paid for I prayed that it would help him, help us, help everything. He had acted so motivated when I told him I was going to leave him that I really thought that he just might make it. He was also smart enough to realize what he had lost out by losing his well-paying job with benefits. He was hopeful that he could get it back if he proved that he completed a program. I assume he tried, but he didn't even attend for longer than three weeks before giving up. I hate him for that reason, but I also understand because there were many times in my life where I wasn't ready for help either. So many of those programs are what start getting individuals on the right track though. He just wasn't ready for the help though, and was drinking on his way home even after the meetings. Naturally out of my normal instincts of double checking to tell whether or not he was telling the truth, I drove by the parking lot one night to see if he was at the meeting as he had said he would be. He wasn't. He came home drunk that night, as I knew he would be, and I started packing the children's and my belongings, even though we didn't have any where to go that exact day.

I asked Ryan to leave. I told him I could be in a different residence with the kids within a month. Of course he screamed at me, and pointed out that everything was my fault and that I would never make it. He argued that it was all my fault. I openly accepted that it was. I was past the point of arguing. He yelled that I was on his ass about everything and that there was nothing wrong with him or his drinking. I didn't care to argue anymore. I had already heard enough of the, "I'm sorrys, it won't happen again, I never meant to hurt you, I'll get help," and every other imaginable curse and excuse, so his last resort was yelling about it. He yelled urgently that I was making a mistake and he would be sure that I regretted it. I felt numb, so I didn't cry, argue, sulk, or rejoice. I was just numb and wanted him out. Finally he left. I changed the locks. He was gone and I was safe. He left us alone… until every other night or so when he broke in despite the new locks. He would drink however often he wanted after I asked him to leave, so he was constantly drunk and didn't even need to try to cover it. He would continue to come over and break in to torment me. My family worked together to move my children and I out even faster. My family had us out of the house within the same week that Ryan was doing that. The house would be put on the market to sell immediately.

Before the adoption had been final for half a year, and before Anna was even three months old, we were clearly separated and living in different residences; he at his mother's house, and me, Taylor, and Anna at my mother's rental house. Sure I was scared, but at least I knew I was safe. My family did so much for me, and I didn't even know it at the time. They helped me escape from what would've turned into an even more dangerous situation as Ryan continued to get into the locked house and continued to drink and rage. Noel stayed with her mother. We were all finally safe!…or so I thought. Considering the circumstantial drama that had been going on for a few years in my life, it really was hard to determine if it was my problems or his problems that were haunting me. That doesn't excuse my lack of response to my own mental health sooner, but it was such a strong matrix between Ryan and I of denial, lies, unknowing, anger, arguments, hate, and hurt that it was easy to be distracted by the same emotions without even considering it to be an illness I had.

In reference to my mental illnesses, which were still undiagnosed and unmedicated, I struggled with *everything*. I struggled being as effective as I could've been at work, my relationship with Taylor suffered as I was on a much more rapid roller coaster. Noel was a teenager and old enough to want to be independent, but I know I could have been a better stepmother to her too. I just always felt too fast or too low. I couldn't ever make heads of tails. I was always one way or the other. I was either the perfect mom baking cookies and playing with the kids, or I was retreating to my room to lie in bed for hours at a time, completely disregarding life. My personalities, of course, altered too. One moment I truly cared, and the other moment the other person in me admitted that I might as well give up. My anxiety of a scale of one to ten felt like it was about a twelve. I couldn't *not* panic. I couldn't *not* worry. I didn't always feel this way though. I don't remember it being such an influence when I was younger, but as I have aged, apparently the anxiety has too. It didn't matter if I loved Ryan or not, I was smart enough to know that the lives of my children depended on my health and my leaving him. It didn't matter if I could hold my emotions together from day to day, I knew that this was just one more opportunity where I would have o develop more disguises. I just knew that after years of dating and loving, it would only take me weeks to break free and escape.

Memorable Moments

I was on a swim team nearly my entire life. I was as comfortable underwater as I was above water. I worked and trained hard, but had a natural and obvious gift too. My family were always huge supporters of my swimming. We had regularly scheduled swim meets, more out of town than local. We rarely ever missed one. It wasn't mandatory participation, but my mom knew that I loved them, so we always went no matter how much the gas, hotel, food, and other travel costs were. It never even stopped her from going when we had to leave or return at outrageous times like one a.m or four a.m. She would drive, while I slept, and always made sure that I had the best training coaches, equipment, suits, goggles, and accessories.

Since I swam as part of a National organization, there were goals established for all of the different races based on the swimmers speed. You would earn a B patch for a good time, an A patch for an even better time, and the A's would go all the way up to AAA for nearly the fastest time possible. Each team member had a jacket where we proudly showed off our patches. As soon as I earned a patch, my mom was up that night after putting my brother and I in bed so that it would be ready for me to show off the next day.

I remember that when I swam, I could hear my family cheering for me at the end of the lane. They cheered for me when I won, and they cheered for me when I was so slow that I could barely finish. Everyone came as often as they could, and swimming is a sport with frequent competitions.

Should've Known Better

Some things never change.
She thought she was stronger.
Saying no was too hard.
Now her pain lasts even longer.
She thought she could leave
her problems behind,
but she found out that his love
was cruel, addicted, and unkind.
She thought he was different
and that she wouldn't get hurt,
but she should've known better
because this wasn't a first

Age 24

CHAPTER 4

House For Sale!

* restrictions apply: <u>not</u> to be used by seller as a <u>whore</u> <u>house</u>.

*E*ven though we were obviously getting a divorce, Ryan and I were civil enough to agree to the terms of the sale of the house. We were pretty agreeable about everything because he didn't want anything. He didn't want the children. He didn't want the house (and couldn't have afforded it anyways). When it came to personal belongings, he just didn't want anything. I don't know if it was because he didn't care or if it was because he didn't think the divorce was really going to happen, or maybe he had an altogether different reason of his own, but he didn't even want even one picture of the kids. I took everything, which wasn't really all that much in monetary value to begin with, but I left out marriage owning all the pictures and memorabilia of our history and our children's. He wanted the ladder, the grill, and his two surfboards. Not that I would've wanted to give him more, but it was somewhat saddening that he didn't want anything representative of the ten years that we were together.

A part of me wished that I would've been able to afford the house on my own, so at least I would've still had something to call my own, but that just wasn't possible. Ryan wouldn't have qualified to keep it on his own based on his job termination and new lower income. He wanted it initially and for a short time we argued about it, but he never stuck by anything, so eventually he gave up on that fight too. Nonetheless when it came to agreeing on the terms of the sale of the house, I think we both just wanted out since the marriage was too damaged and beyond repair. We were both ready to sell the house, but Ryan wanted to do it without any effort. The difference between us was that I knew the work that had to be put into a house to sell it in a tough market, and I actually cared somewhat (although just barely) about getting it done. Ryan didn't seem at all concerned about fixing the house so that it would sell more quickly. He only wanted to hang on to it temporarily to do the things he wanted to hide, and then just let it go whenever it sold. I hated the hassle of all of it, but it seemed like Ryan didn't care about selling the house at all. He had been fired and didn't have an idea or care as to how he was going to pay his half until it sold, but still didn't care.

My mother and I spent hours cleaning, scrubbing, painting, repairing, and preparing the house for presentation. Ryan avoided the work completely, and simply stated, that he just didn't care. I wish I could say that I was grateful for my mom's help, but truth be told, I resented her for wanting to fix it up and making me help (even though she didn't really "make me"). We argued frequently because I hated even being in the house, let alone doing work on it. I argued about having to paint it. She justified that it would make it look better. I argued about fixing some of the things I considered to be minor, but my mom tackled the project the only way she knew how; she's a perfectionist. My mom's husband helped with the work. My uncle, brother, dad, grandfather, grandmother…my family all pitched in to help prepare for the sale of a house that wasn't even their responsibility. It's easier for me to be grateful now, but at the time I resented it all. I absolutely detested any and all of the work I did, even though my mom really did most of the work. I think I was just too low, circumstantially and with my bipolar that I hated her even for doing it, let alone making me help too. One personality distinctively took over very easily, however truthful it may have felt. The constantly angry, frustrated, mean, uncaring, and dangerously spontaneous side of me took over, and I loved hating so much. I was so low that the old adage "misery loves company" really was true. I felt miserable. I looked miserable. My life was miserable, and I wanted to make everyone else as miserable as I was. Yes I was happy to be leaving such a bad marriage and was relieved about that, but it's not like that's exactly what I wanted my life to be like.

I was angry at Ryan. I was frustrated that my family was creating extra work for me, when in reality I had created more work for them. I was overwhelmingly annoyed with Taylor and Anna because I was trying to manage two houses, raise them the best I could, juggle finances that just weren't working, and follow through with the divorce paperwork. I felt this way for months. Since I was the one who wanted out of the divorce as quickly as possible, I told Ryan that I would cover all of the costs. That meant extra work to earn the extra money. I worked overtime, relying on my family to juggle my kids. I was frustrated at that, but it was worth it if it meant getting our of a bad marriage sooner. No matter the fact that I was going in the right direction though, I was angry, frustrated, and depressed.

While the divorce was easily progressing through the paperwork system, Ryan drank, did drugs, had sex with a pregnant teenager girl, and eventually bragged to me about all of it. She called out the window of her parent's home one night as he was driving by, and they were having sex an hour later. He didn't even care that she was obviously very pregnant with another man's baby, let alone waiting until the divorce was final. I wasn't hurt over the actual act of sex, but I'll admit, I was crushed that he didn't honor the vows promised before God at least until the divorce was final. When we were discussing the divorce papers, he easily relinquished all rights to the children, and he had already let me take everything, so there really wasn't much left to do other than sign the papers once they were completed. He even bragged about living every man's dream; having sex with a girl as young as his teenage daughter without any commitments! That is how he spoke of it. My family spent thousands of dollars, replacing the carpet and dishwasher, purchasing cleaning and painting supplies, and everything that could've been potentially needed to sell the house. They made sure it was taken care of. I was falling apart, so once again, my family stuck up for me and held me together like glue.

Within a month the house was ready to be put on the market. Ryan and I signed the papers with the realtor, and hoped and prayed that someone would take the bait and buy the house. A month went by and no interested buyers, so we lowered the price. Another month went by, and the realtor called to say that neighbors were complaining because Ryan hadn't been cutting the small front yard, as he had committed to doing. Since I had both kids and was actually working full time too, Ryan had said that he would maintain the yard. Since the day we put the house on the market, he only cut the grass once. After the particular complaint I somehow managed to get someone to watch both of my kids, got a lawnmower over there, cut the grass, and cleaned out any debris that was nearby. Even all that effort was easier than asking, begging, and threatening Ryan to do it when I knew, in the end, that he wouldn't have done it anyways.

Another month, no sale, and no offers. Again, we lowered the price. The realtor suggested that we try to make it look more "homey" so mom and I went to the store and purchased hand towels and soap holders, dish towels, candles, and anything else we could think of to make the house seem more like a home. We went to the house and immediately started setting everything up. That's when I noticed the drawer full of condoms; some opened and empty, and others still unused and in their packages. Thanks Ryan! Here my family had been working so hard to sell the house and work with the reality, and my husband was just using it as his personal whore house. Realtors leave their business cards when they come to visit a home. On my way out the door, I left with a stack of condoms and business cards. It was bad enough that I noticed all the beer and liquor bottles around whenever I stopped by there for a routine cleaning, but finding his stash of condoms was another story. Of course I called him and told him that he could do whatever he wanted to do, JUST NOT in the house we were trying to SELL!

Still no offers, so we again lowered the price. This time it was a lesser amount than the amount that we even owed, so I started getting scared. How were we going to pay the difference? How were we going to keep up with payments since my savings was finally dried up? How were we even going to sell it at all? How would we be able to pay the realtor? I felt hopeless. Every time I called the mortgage company with questions, they kept trying to find a way that I could keep the house. The only payment I could afford on my own was about half of what they offered me as a payment plan. I couldn't count on Ryan helping deal with the mortgage company, so I dealt with all their threats and curt conversations and letters in the mail by myself. It just felt like they weren't listening when I told them that I couldn't do it. If I tried to push them to talk about foreclosure or other more positive alternatives, but they acted like it wasn't possible and that I would be financially tied to a house I couldn't afford until the day I died. It wasn't a good time to sell if you even wanted to break even. The market was extremely low. Then, a hopeful moment when the realtor called! I will never forget. I was sitting in the Doctor's office waiting to be seen when she called.

At first I was excited, then the purpose and the tone of the conversation set in. More complaints, and as always, related to

Ryan. The realtor kindly explained to me that when a fellow realtor showed the house to prospective buyers, he and the couple were shocked to see used condoms lying on the floor (in the room that had previously been Taylor's bedroom). This would be when I dubbed the residence "The House of Adultery and Sin." Even though we weren't officially divorced yet, after the separation, I had initially and wrongfully assumed that Ryan would honor the vows of marriage and be respectful until the swift divorce was completed, just as an act of kindness and formality. Even though I had seen the evidence of Ryan's activities in the drawer previously and knew of his involvement with the pregnant teenage girl, never in a million years did I expect a call from my realtor asking me to kindly stop by the house and dispose of his used evidence. Ryan didn't care about throwing used condoms and wrappers away it when he committed the act, so why bother calling and demanding that he clean it up now. He wouldn't have because he simply didn't care.

I was so shocked and embarrassed that I rescheduled my appointment for another day and rushed to clean up the house. I was mortified. How could he? I was so frustrated that I cried the whole drive over to the house. Not because I was hurt, but because all my emotions were going too fast all at once. I was offended that he didn't have the courtesy to wait until the divorce was final. Moreover, I was cruelly hurt by having to clean up the mess of his unfaithfulness. I was horrified that I would have to continue working with this realtor because, like the mortgage company, Ryan wasn't involved and didn't care. I was just so overwhelmed with emotions, and had no outlet. It was just one more opportunity for him to cause me pain, and of course, it did. There was no telling what else Ryan had left behind too. All this even though he didn't even have a key since I had changed the locks before I even moved out. However, it is kind of hard to press trespassing charges or breaking and entering charges on your husband when you are co-owners of the property.

As I walked in the front door of the house, I felt the horror of the act that had been committed in the house where my daughter was conceived. The house where my son had been adopted/born to. The first house that I could ever call my home, as it was the first house I had ever purchased. It was the first house where Noel was allowed to choose her own room paint colors and decorations. So many firsts were accomplished in that house. How could he be so callous about a home that once signified so much, I wondered silently. Even though the realtor told me where they were, I knew I would need to search other places as well, just to be sure. I started my search. I searched the downstairs rooms first and threw away the random condom wrappers that were astray and scattered on the floor. I checked the kitchen drawers, more unused condoms, but nothing else out of the ordinary. I threw the few beers that were in the fridge away. Finally the assent upstairs. It felt like every step was like climbing a mountain since I already knew what I would find. I checked the room we used to laugh and love in; our bedroom. No condoms yet though. I checked Noel's abandoned room, and still found nothing. I already knew, but I stopped just outside of Taylor's old room from the time he was three to the time he was five before I entered.

There they were. Three used, limp, filled, dried up condoms on the floor of Taylor's old bedroom. My imagination ran rampant with visions of Ryan and another woman. I was startled at my anger over the horror of the actions he had taken in our son's bedroom. It felt sacrilegious. How could someone have meaningless sex with a woman he didn't even know in the bedroom where we had raised our son. I couldn't move as memories of playing board games in that very bedroom with Taylor flashed through my mind. I stood motionless as the memories of watching t.v., completing puzzles, and reading books together in that room clouded my mind. Then, just as soon as it came on, the memories vanished. I quickly cleaned up the mess as fast as I could and left. When I locked the front door, I knew it would be for the last time. I knew I would never have the mental strength to ever walk through those doors again. Regardless of whether or not the house would sell, I would never again return to "The House of Adultery and Sin".

I was insulted, by yet, one more violation upon me as a person. Violated again, but in a different way this time, as opposed to the fun Ryan had with his camera. At this point, I again to began to question beginnings because I sure the hell couldn't figure out how I had gotten to the point of picking up my soon-to-be ex husband's used condoms! Although not an actual psychological "flashback" as known to medical terminology, at this point, I had to ask myself, "how the hell did I wind up here?" "At what point did my decline begin?" My mind went back through the puzzle pieces of my life to try to decide where exactly when, where, and how I had made my mistake that led me here, and how to find a new beginning to repair my mistake. Somewhere there had to be an ending to my pain, which also meant that I was supposed to get a fresh start new beginning. When did I begin to decline? Had I *ever* had a happy beginning to at all? Would the pain ever end long enough so that I could repair my damaged soul and still be capable of having a happy new beginning? What if this was my life, no new beginnings and no happiness? Just roller coasters and inner demons? As I stood in that room cleaning up behind Ryan's evidence of adultery, I stopped long enough to think back over many years. One year ago. Five years ago. Ten years ago. I thought back as far as I could…

Memorable Moments

Since my daughter is so young, we are just at the beginning of starting memories together. One thing about her that I will never be able to forget is how much of a girly-girl she has been ever since she was born. She always insisted that she pick out the clothes that she wanted to wear. She constantly wanted her toenails painted pink. She has three dresser drawers for shoes! Can you believe any two year old would care enough about shoes that she actually has that many drawers for shoes? She is my princess who loves wearing frilly dresses that "swish" to school, has to be the one to pick her own hair ribbons, and gets frustrated when I don't let her take her purse to school.

I'll never forget though the warmth I feel when she looks into my eyes and says, "hold you." It's not for my convenience either. She loves patent leather shoes, glittery sparkly shoes, dress up princess shoes, and any other type of unique trendy shoe. Coming from someone who only has half of the girly-girl gene, since I never got too big in the nail polish and make up, my precious angelic beauty queen daughter will always keep me smiling about her particulars. Believe it or not, she has even insisted that she wear some of her favorite shoes at night!

I Wish

Sometimes I wish
that they could see
the feelings I have
hidden in me.
Sometimes I wish
I could let it all out
be the person I am
within and without.
Sometimes I wish
that I had nothing to hide,
no hurtful secrets
and no reason to cry

Age 9

CHAPTER 5

I'm Sorry I Didn't Tell You Sooner Mommy

Somewhere in all the questioning I had over the deterioration of my life (or so it felt) I began to travel back in time to try to discover when and where exactly I fell apart. If I could pinpoint that moment, I could make the changes I needed and then have a new beginning. Or at least that's what I hoped for. I just hated the thought that this was as good as it gets, so that is why reaching a new beginning felt so important to me. As an adult, I began to think back about my younger years. I had, like most children, wonderful and exciting moments as well as sad moments. So far I figured I must have been normal enough, so was I just already strategizing on how to fit in? Is that how I appeared so normal? I was mischievous, bright, had several talents, and felt all the love in the world from my family. Not to suggest that I was always completely normal though, for whatever normal is. Even a few family stories told about my toddler years point out my distinct differences from other toddlers my age. I did everything on time, but was just "different." Nonetheless when I was four I was molested. I'm not sure if this fits into my life story, or if it fits into my mental illnesses story, but I also don't have very many memories of before I was four either. I'm not sure why, other than his threats, but the day it happened when my mom picked me up I acted as if it was like any other typical day. I did not tell her. I already knew that it was a secret in my soul that I would always keep buried. Five years later when I was nine, I decided, for whatever reasons, that I *had* to tell her.

I remember the drive as clearly as if it happened yesterday. My mom, my baby brother, and I were driving home, and the butterflies in my stomach were lurching around madly. I knew I had to tell my mom, but I just couldn't get the words out. It felt like the words would form in my mind, but get lost in my mouth before I could actually say anything. By now I was old enough to know that it was wrong. I tried, but every time I said, "mommy…," then I would just say something else insignificant. I chocked back the words because admitting it to her would hurt her, but it was also a final admission that it had hurt me too. We didn't exactly have far to travel but it seemed like the car was racing. We were driving too fast and getting home too quickly. I do not know why this is the time that I committed myself to confessing to my mom, but it was the time limit that I had imposed upon myself. I don't even know why I felt the urgency or reason of importance for her telling her now, but I just knew that I had to do it. I had to admit to my mistake. "Mommy, I'm sorry I didn't tell you sooner, but a bad man made me touch him in his private place and then he touched my private place too. I'm sorry." I wasn't ready to tell her yet that he made me try oral sex with him, but at least I had opened the doorway to the truth. That much made me feel released from the chains of guilt that I was bound by.

My mom was speechless for what seemed like an eternity,

but I know that her silence was only because her heart couldn't handle the thought of her daughter being hurt and violated in the horrific way that I was. When she spoke, her concern was loaded with questions. When? Who? It's ok now, so don't be scared. Where? It's not your fault, so don't be sorry. How? Did another adult know who could've protected me? I love you. She peppered a million supportive words and angry questions about the perpetrator. She was furious that I had proven that she hadn't been able to protect me as well as she had tried to. She was furious that she couldn't save her precious baby from the dangers that lurked the world. She didn't ask what she could do to help me, but I wouldn't have known anyways. Years later she admitted that one of her friends recommended therapy which we did not follow through on for whatever reasons; however, I know one of mom's regrets is on not having taken me to a therapist. It wouldn't have changed my later diagnoses, but it could have made some of the years and trauma in my life easier if either of us had an understanding of the implications of childhood sexual abuse.

If I had to guess why we didn't follow through on the therapy suggestion, it was probably at my insistence. I probably didn't feel like I needed it, but then again, I probably didn't exactly understand what "therapy" was. I cannot remember exactly why we chose not to go. If that isn't the reason then it is because I had waited so long to tell my mom that we both assumed that it had left me unscarred, or that I was over the emotional damage by now. Since I don't have any other possible logical reason that comes to mind about why I waited so long to tell my mom, maybe the molestation didn't hurt me as much as the damage that I already felt inside me. I had always felt that difference between me and other children, so being molested probably isn't what changed me. I never wanted to tell anyone how I felt inside before either because I knew it was bad, so I certainly wasn't going to ever include that in any conversation.

It seemed like my mom and I talked once about the man

molesting me, admitted that it happened, and then let it go as we moved on with our lives. I'm not sure that it happened exactly that simplistically, but it felt like it to me. It was awkward for me to talk about since I was getting older and more aware of my own body, and I'm sure if was painful for her to ask questions, It seemed like we were walking on eggshells around it. My answers hurt her. My memories plagued me. It just felt like that was the end of it and that there was nothing that could be done about it now. Although my memory may not be correct, I do not think we even talked about it again until many years and problems later.

The particular incident occurred only once when I was four. I had a regular babysitter who watched me after my morning preschool program, and she loved me as she did her own children. There were so many positive lessons I learned there about academics, social play, and even life in general. Once I stole a ceramic decoration from her bathroom. Instead of yelling or scolding me, we talked about it together so that I understood why I shouldn't take things that didn't belong to me. She made peanut butter and marshmallow fluff sandwiches, which I hated, but taught me that you are rewarded when you do what you know you are supposed to do rather than pitch a fit against following rules. I learned patience by her teaching me that even if I wasn't tired, my body still needed a few minutes of rest. She didn't scold me when I got up, just hugged me and reminded me that I needed to rest a little longer. She never threatened me about not sleeping. She only allowed me to watch t.v. programs that were educational, and only for a limited time. We played with toys and games, and just had a fun time together. I didn't realize how much I had learned from her until I got older.

On rare occasions though, she had to make another appointment and was unable to watch me. During these times, I usually went to the "stand in" babysitter that other kids I knew also went to. She did her babysitting from her home, just as my routine babysitter did. The "stand in" babysitter was nice enough, made the best jelly sandwiches, and had lots of toys. Her house was always in disarray though, clothes and toys left astray and misplaced, and the highchair left dirty with scattered bits of food. We generally seemed to be allowed to keep to ourselves as long as we "left the adults alone". She did not have a routine like my normal baby sitter so I was a little uncomfortable not knowing when and what we would be doing, but I went along with it. As different as I may have been, I was easily enough well behaved so that my behavior was never a problem. The only part of her routine I knew was that after lunch, we had to take a nap until she told us we could get up. Sometimes it seemed like she made us take extra long naps, but I knew enough about her mannerisms to know not to approach her like I would've my regular babysitter. Apparently the stand in babysitter had to leave momentarily while we were taking our naps. I don't know if this was a frequent habit of hers or not, but on this day it changed me.

During my nap, I woke up to use the restroom. I was already intimidated because I knew she did not like us "bothering the adults" when it was our nap times, but I quietly tiptoed to the bathroom. I wasn't worried about what was going to happen when I got there. I just wanted to get there without getting in trouble. Since I was only four, I was potty trained, but I remember the effort it still took to get my own "big girl" panties off and climb on and off the seemingly huge toilet seat. As I was finishing using the restroom, the teenage son of the babysitter came into the obviously occupied bathroom. I didn't know enough to be suspicious, so when he offered to help, I innocently thought that he was just being helpful and nice. He helped me off the toilet, but instead of helping to pull my panties up, he pulled them down to around my ankles. He kindly told me that he wanted to touch me. Ok, I thought, adults touch me all the time when they pick me up, hug me, buckle my seat belt, and many other times. He explained that he was going to touch my girly private place because I would like it and he would show me how. He said he would like it too and I would get in trouble if I didn't make him happy. It wasn't that I wanted to please him, but I didn't want to get in trouble with his mom (the stand in babysitter) or my mom either.

At first he was testing his limits to see if I would tell him no, but again, I was to naïve, innocent, and unknowing to know that I was *supposed* to say no. It didn't feel good, but then again, neither did getting a shot or getting sick. It didn't feel right, but he said it wasn't wrong. I didn't know that this was any different than any other kind of pain. At first he just gently touched me. Being a teenager, I think he was scared too, but he still certainly knew better! He parted me slightly and then touched the outer areas of my "girly parts," as he called them. He rubbed his fingers around and tried to push them inside me, all the while claiming that this was how girls were supposed to make themselves feel good. He barely put his fingers inside, but it was enough to make me slightly yelp and squirm away. He encouraged me to do more by reassuring me that it was ok. He kept his head so low and near to my body, that I thought he was looking to see if I was doing something right or wrong. Little did I know that he was watching because he was getting off on seeing what he was doing to me. He said that it was good, but that I should not tell anyone because they might get mad at me for doing it.

Once he had his fill of torturing me by touching and fingering my delicate body, he pulled his pants down and stuck his hard penis in my face. "This is what a boy looks like," he proudly said. No sense of regret in his voice; just pride that he was going to temporarily possess a little girl to get off on. "Touch it," he urged. I tried to back away. So quickly and so hard that I was forced back down onto the toilet seat lid and backed up against the back of the toilet. My panties and shorts were still around my ankles, one shoe had fallen off, and I didn't know what I was supposed to do. I knew that I hadn't liked what he had done to me, but I also knew that I wasn't supposed to tell anyone too. I had nowhere to go. He towered over me. I was scared, I couldn't get out, and no one would hear me scream! "Touch it," he commanded more hoarsely this time as he grabbed my hand and clamped it around himself. I had no idea what I was doing as he held his hand over my hand and moved it back and forth over himself. I just wanted it to end.

I felt scared, but I still didn't *know* that it was wrong. At this point, I didn't care how to make myself feel good (as he had claimed it would) and I certainly had no interest in knowing what a boy looked like. I wasn't interested in them before, and I definitely wasn't interested in them locked in the bathroom with a stranger molesting me. When he finished showing off himself by making me awkwardly jerk him off, he told me to kiss it (meaning his penis). I barely leaned forward, but he pushed my head down and made me kiss it. I didn't like that it felt wet. "Now practice like it was a piece of candy you are sucking on," he urged. I didn't move. He used his hands to help open my mouth, and actually led my face down to his dick as if I hadn't understood what he said. I understood it perfectly fine. I just didn't want to do it. How do you tell a grown up no though without getting in trouble, I thought. The only good moment was when he reprimanded me and said, "get out of here and go take a nap," after he finished briefly making me give him oral sex.

I don't know why I waited nearly five years to tell my mom. I believed his threat as a young child, but for some reason I waited until I was much older to tell her even after I knew that his threats were just harmless words. For many years, even though I knew I was different from other children, I did not think of this particular incident and I didn't relate my difference to it. I can honestly say that I nearly forgot about it, so it wasn't exactly a battle of personal wills on whether or not to tell her. Still I do not know why the wait, and I cannot say if it made me feel any better or not. I just didn't realize how mixed up I was about it. My admission to my mom couldn't change that, and no one could've interpreted from my admission to her that I was mentally damaged or not.

Years later I found out that my parents had more than one near run in with the family of the son. Since my parents would never send me to someone's house that they didn't know, they obviously knew exactly where the woman and her son lived. Both my mom and dad drove by their house, pulled up to the curb or in the driveway, and had a "coming to Jesus" with themselves about revenge. They would sit there and envision the torture I had endured in that tiny, dirty, dingy bathroom. They imagined their precious daughter being so cruelly abused, knowing that I didn't even have full realm of understanding at the time. They would entertain visions of bloody revenge! How dare anyone ever hurt their baby angel! Fortunately neither of them ever stepped out of the car, so life went on as best as it could. None of us even realized how much it still impacted me though. It wouldn't be until I was damaged even more before we would realize that it had been a problem for me, in some capacity, all along. It wasn't the biggest issue that I had to deal with, but it was a skeleton in my closet nonetheless that had apparently been haunting me for a while.

Memorable Moments

My dad and I shared a special unique bond because we both loved NASCAR. If I had a nickel for every perfect moment I had with my dad at NASCAR races, I would be a billionaire by now. I'll never forget the first race we ever went to together, as well as all the others too.

At the time, we just considered ourselves the luckiest people in the world to even be going to Talladega for the race for a sport that we both loved. Our seats were terrible, our parking space was horrific, and the drive back was the worst in the slowest moving traffic possible, but that was the perfect beginning for us; we were hooked.

We've been to the Bristol Motor Speedway, stood in the pits with the drivers, and ridden around the track with drivers. We toured the pits and walked the track of Talladega, watched the pre race set ups at several tracks, screamed with crowds at the final race in Homestead, and were moved by the power behind the Daytona 500 race. As I mentioned, I'd be rich if I had a nickel for every positive moment I had at the tracks with my dad. So what was the best part about it? We had our own NASCAR language that no one else understood (unless they were also a fan, and there weren't any others in my family who felt as drawn to NASCAR), and when we went, it just my daddy and me! How lucky can a girl possibly get?

Behind Closed Doors

I'll show you mine
if you show me yours.
No one will know
if you close all the doors.
It can't be wrong
but just don't tell.
You'll get in trouble.
I've been told that as well.
I was told that before.
When he asked me to try.
So don't worry at all...
It will be fun? – maybe he was right?

Age 9

CHAPTER 6

Curious Innocence or Sexual Bossiness?

Even at a young age, I was smart enough to know that I was different from other children. I had also learned how to manipulate well and how to use my disguises and personalities interchangeably when it came to dealing with friends or authority figures. I didn't want anyone to notice how darkly disturbed I was, so I constantly tried to cover it up. Many children go through a "playing Doctor" phase. I made sure that I hid this phase from my mom (my parents were divorced by now) because I knew I was going beyond the normal limits of the typical Doctor play. I don't know why I wanted to do it. I don't know why I did it. I don't know why none of my friends ever questioned it. I don't know why the thought of it even occurred to me, but regardless of all the things I didn't know, there was one thing that I did know. I liked it, however weird and unknown my reasons for doing it may have been.

It first started innocently enough in my kindergarten class. I got in trouble for French kissing another boy in my class behind the slide one day. It wasn't because I liked the boy or wanted him to be my "boyfriend" or anything, I was just turned on by doing something I knew I wasn't supposed to do. This was actually at the school where my grandmother taught, so even my fear of upsetting her couldn't deter my inner demons that constantly tugged and raised my roller coaster. I played piano, swam competitively, did well in school, and spent a lot of time with my family, but I still knew I was different. I cussed out my great grandmother about a sweater. Granted it was the first time I had ever used those words, so I could get away with saying that I didn't know that they were bad words, but I most certainly did know. I was just that spontaneously angry when she told me to put it on and couldn't not say it.

My emotions were always a roller coaster, even when it came to simple things, but there weren't any consequences that deterred me from trying to be promiscuous with my friends. It my first or second grade birthday party. I can't remember exactly what year it was because at the time our classrooms all had two grades within them. We would do first grade with one teacher on one half of the room and second grade with the other teacher on the other side of the room, so we all knew each other anyways. I think I probably invited everyone from both classes, and even my neighborhood friends too. I can still see the picture of it all in my mind now. My small townhouse was clustered with friends, family, and presents. All the kids had birthday hats and half of them were running around madly playing a game of tag in the backyard. We even played some of the more calm games that we played in school just because we thought it would be fun. It was, and appeared to be a normal birthday party. We had cake and ice cream, I had torn through the presents, millions of pictures had been taken, and the guests had finally left. It was a great party! We had played birthday party games, played on the swing set and in the play house, and just had a great time overall. I even remember that my favorite picture from that party was taken right as I was jumping out of the swing. I looked so happy and innocent. I was, except that I was darkly disturbed and deeply damaged already too. My mom must have been exhausted, but I was thrilled to be having my first school friend ever spend the night with me. All the guests had left, except my best friend who would be staying overnight.

While my mom was in the house cleaning up, and taking a few quick minutes to sit down every now and then, my friend and I were playing safely in the backyard. We were dodging daddy long leg spiders that liked to roost on the top of my playhouse, and running back and forth from the house to get baby dolls and plastic toy dishes. We were determined this was going to be the real thing. We were going to take care of our baby in a REAL house, since it was after all, a real life sized playhouse. What more could any young child ask for? Once we had everything we needed and all the snacks possible, we both instantly became mommy to our new baby in the house. We had dishes to cook food for her and for ourselves, and everything we needed to take care of ourselves, until inevitably one of us had to go to the bathroom.

At first it was just funny to pee in a cup and then dump it out the playhouse window. We'd go back inside, refill our other drinking cups with juice, and then head back out hoping to pee again as soon as possible. She didn't mind it, but I *really* liked it. It wasn't seeing her naked that excited me. It was the dirtiness of seeing her do something I knew we shouldn't do that enticed me as I ascended in my own young mania. It was taking turns seeing each other that thrilled me. It was seeing places on each other that we both knew we weren't supposed to see that enthralled me. It was fun, but beyond the realm of normal "Doctor" play. Despite "Doctor" play being a normal phase, my version was for all the wrong reasons even though the act itself may have only seemed gross or unusual.

The rest of the evening was uneventful, but at bedtime I

decided to press my luck with my friend even further. What was she willing to do? What was I willing to do? Not sexually together, but I definitely wanted to do things that I clearly had enough sense to know that we shouldn't do. I assume my reasons were because of the early childhood sexual molestation experience, or because of the unmedicated mind suffering from mental illnesses, but only because I can't think of any other logical reason why I did it. I just knew that I wanted to test the limits of sexual curiosity and bossiness, not because I was attracted to her, but because I thrived on learning, doing and seeing more. My interest was certainly over exaggerated than that of other children of the same age, but for some reason, it was a need I felt.

As common with other friendly spend the nights, we both dressed in our pajamas and crawled into bed. Of course it felt like two a.m., but I'm sure it was probably only ten p.m. or so. As soon as I was sure that my mom was out of earshot and otherwise occupied watching t.v. in her own room, I started talking to my friend about sexual topics. I explained to her how I masturbated, even though I didn't even know what I was doing, what it was really called, or what the feeling was that I felt afterwards. Rolling up the sheets and positioning myself so that my vagina was over the bulge of the sheets, I showed her how I pressed the sheets into my clit and then rolled back and forth until it led me into a childhood orgasm. The best part though, I must admit, was talking her into doing it and watching her too. Still to this day, I don't know the exact reason why I did it other than mental illness and past experiences.

That only added flame to my curiosity, and I plunged deeper into my sexual drive, despite how young I still was. Even though I knew it was wrong, I wasn't sure why it was wrong, and it made me so manic that I probably wouldn't have cared anyways. Even though it would take years before a correct diagnosis was reached, I have probably been destined to be bipolar. With a flashlight in hand, I prompted my friend, "wouldn't it be fun to look at each other *down there?*" We plotted a plan that we were comfortable with, and I went first. She crept under the covers with the flashlight, as I spread myself for her to get a closer glimpse. When it was my turn to see her, I couldn't tell if I was more excited showing her my body, looking at her body, or the mischievous excitement of doing something sexual that we could get in trouble for. I didn't know at the time why I felt these urges. It wasn't because I was attracted to members of my own sex, I just didn't have any access to boys yet. I was dark and twisty, and when my first friend wasn't opposed to it, it only encouraged me to try with other friends too.

I wish that I could say that this only happened once, but in all honesty, every slumber party I was invited to, it was always my game suggestion when we laid down for the night. The older I got, the more daring I got. I had to have that nightly childhood orgasm, and I did it every night at home. It was a ritual that felt good, but I was still to young to even know why. Nonetheless, at every spin the night I had, I always tried to convince my friends to do the same thing for three reasons: one, I wanted to see and experiment with them, and two because I couldn't disrupt my routine of my nightly orgasms, and three, because it confirmed that I wasn't "crazy" since none of my friends ever rejected my suggestions.

Even regular friendly gatherings I went to, I still tried to manipulate my way into playing a game that had a sexual orientation. Even if it wasn't a bedtime game, we would dress our Barbies and pay careful attention to their anatomy and then compare it to our own and each other's. We would dress up for what we called talent shows in our bedrooms that were more representative of childhood stripper shows, to be honest with you. We would strut around purposefully so that we could see one another nearly naked. It was always my encouragement that kept the game going. I was, and am, a leader, and truth be told, I wasn't bad at manipulating to get whatever I wanted. Regardless of whether or not it was a party or just one of my other friends and myself, I couldn't stop thinking about the forbidden body parts of boys and girls. I wanted to think about it. I wanted to see it. I wanted to read it. I wanted to draw it. I wanted to soak it all in, even though I knew I too young to receive much of that information from my parents.

Memorable Moments

When I was four, my parents took me to Sea World. I remember the thrilling feelings I had just walking into the park. At Sea World, one of our obvious stops was to see Shamu at the Whale Show. That was the main attraction for every visitor, me especially. I couldn't wait to see a real live whale! Never in my life had I seen anything more than pictures of whales. On the way to our seats (probably an hour early because I was driving my parents crazy about seeing the show) we grabbed some popcorn, ice cream, and drinks. By the end of our meal, I was covered in food – typical for any youngster.

The next thing we knew, we were being approached by one of the general managers. I was a kid in paradise, so I didn't care what the grown ups had to talk about. My eyes quickly scanned the surroundings; the glistening water, the posters of marine animals, the banners and billboards of other aquatic life, there was so much to take in. The conversation with the gentleman that my parents met only lasted a few minutes, but it was a few minutes of talking that would give me a fun memory that I would never forget. During the time that they were talking, the manager asked my parents if I would like to participate in the show by being called down at the half way point to actually get to sit on the back of Shamu. Are you kidding? Would I like to? That was bigger than any dream I even had about coming, so of course I definitely wanted to. That left my parents scrambling to buy me a new Sea World shirt since my other one was covered with popcorn, snow cones, ice cream, and every other unimaginable sticky goo while I was so excited that I could hardly sit still.

When the big moment came, it was every bit as exciting and important as I hoped it would be. They announced my name over the loud speaker to come down to the podium where Shamu rested. I stood right beside him before taking a quick seat on his back. Truthfully I was scared, but it created positive memories to last a lifetime.

*I turned this poem in as a school assignment, at age 11, and still no one asked me any questions.

Fate

Shatter the glass.
Kill the child.
Open the doorway,
to free the wild.
Let the winds blow.
Storm the seas.
Dismantle the living,
or whatever be.
Slay the fire.
Quench the dead.
Whiten the eyes,
of blood diamond red.
Beat the winner.
Implode the hate.
Open your mind,
End your own fate.

CHAPTER 7

Passed By And Falling Through The Cracks

I was a great student, as measured by academic standards, but as I continued to develop, so did my bipolar disorder and other mental illnesses. As I mentioned before, in early childhood I appeared as normal as any other child despite the mental illnesses that were lurking inside. I was intelligent, friendly, outgoing, and generally seemed happy. I was obedient, helpful, and always at the top of my class. I was always the winner of several prestigious elementary school awards. Despite my increasingly obvious and very noticeable problems and behaviors, every teacher I had turned their heads and ignored the signs. Due to the abnormalities many people with mental illnesses feel, we become quite adequate at trying to fool others with personalities, moods, and disguises. The disguises often work, unless you are someone who is careful enough to see the truth as it falls through our cracks. Of course I disguised myself as best as I could when I was around others, so it wasn't exactly like I was begging for help, but a lot of indicators of a struggling child were also very present. I was smart enough to use my disguises to cover my moods and personalities so that my parents and friends parents couldn't tell how darkly disturbed I was. I already knew how different I was, I just had to perfect how well I covered it up. My teachers, counselors, and others who were close to me outside of my family noticed on more than one opportunity that something was different. They didn't do anything about it and never spoke up though.

No matter what grade, first through fifth, I was never talked to or monitored the way I should have been. In second and third grades, when I pinched or slapped a friend's butt, I was simply seated out of recess for ten minutes. When I tried to peek under the stall in the girl's restroom in the same grades, I had to pull a behavior card from the chart that put me on my yellow card – no real consequence. I was smart enough to know that. When I got caught in the boy's restroom repeatedly in fourth grade, I was told to go back to class, and most of the time it wasn't even reported to my teacher. I use to hide in the stalls of the boy's restroom, just hoping to catch a glimpse. When I wore shorts or skirts that I knew were too short I would bend over on purpose hoping the boys would look. I know the teachers could see my panties as well as the rest of the class, but it was never mentioned. Although other kids told on me for my explicitly inappropriate words and stories I was still only seated for part of recess.

When babysitters came to our house to baby sit my brother and I as I neared late elementary school and early middle school, it was never a hard task to get them to talk to me about sex. I've since realized that that is the reason why I never had to have much of "the talk" with my mother. I already knew the basics, and probably even more than she would have been ready for me to know. All I had to do to get the babysitters talking was begin by asking innocent, unknowing, and curious questions about my own female anatomy, boys, and relationships. Some of the babysitters cautioned me, but most of them began by answering my questions, and then elaborating on their own experiences. Needless to say, for me and my disturbed mind, it always made a great bedtime story. None of them mentioned it to my mom, and I certainly wasn't going to tell.

At summer day camp, the same thing. I was passed by teachers, despite my silent screaming for help, and now I was being passed over by counselors despite my screaming without a sound. The other kids would be playing sports and game, doing arts and crafts, singing, playing cards, or swimming, and I was hiding to draw sexual pictures, write sexual fantasies, and discretely read books that had sexual content whenever I had the chance. It didn't even have to be a book about sex. Romance novels were good too because I would read and reread the sexual parts practically to the point of memorization. The feeling that reading, talking, or drawing about sex or anatomies was so intensely good. I will never know how I was able to hide all these signs from teachers and counselors for so long. Manipulation, intelligence, and the strong ability to be secretive, I suppose. I will take the blame, rather than suggest that I was "passed by" by many people in the public who were in the position to help me. I would rather blame myself than think that they chose to overlook me when they knew that I was sinking.

Instead of delving further into my real problems, they just turned their heads and looked away. I was never sent to the office. My parents were never called or warned. Not even one teacher brought it to my parents attention. How were my parents supposed to help me work through things if they didn't even know that a problem existed? Here I was in obvious refusal to follow dress code, let alone code of contact and conduct, and my parents were never called. I was never talked to about it by a teacher. I was never talked to it by a principal or guidance counselor. I hope the teachers, counselors, and people in the position to protect kids are more apt at picking up the signs than they were years ago.

When I left elementary school for the world of middle school, I did it with the realization that I was also one of the biggest students. I was one of the heaviest kids in sixth grade. I knew this because we all watched our p.e. coach chart our initial weight so that he could show us our weight loss progress over time. Thanks Coach! Embarrass the fat kid (who is already deeply disturbed) right in front of all her peers! Due to my size, I had a difficult time wearing any jeans. No matter what style I tried, they never fit right in all the places I needed them to. Long story short, I had to go mostly with the stirrup stretchable pants because that was about all that was left that I could wear. When I was smaller nothing could've deterred me from wearing things that were too short or too tight because I loved the attention. I did go through heavy and awkward years though, so it wasn't always about dressing precociously. Since the p.e. weight class incident though, I was mortified and wore things that definitely covered more, but the only pants I could still find for my short length and wide legs was the stretchy stirrups. I was absolutely humiliated and hated myself from without and within at this point!

The one time a teacher ever spoke to me directly about anything out of the ordinary was in sixth grade. She pulled me out of class for a "private conversation." I was already so darkly disturbed that I didn't have any idea which part of me she wanted to dissect and talk about. Most of my turmoil was still disguised, but I had always been silently screaming in my clothes, actions, and misbehaviors, so I really didn't know what to expect. I followed her to the door with sweaty palms because I started to wonder how much of the truth she had been able to see in me. How much had she been able to sense about me already? Could she tell how rotten I was inside? She opened the door and I instinctively turned back to see her behind me before leaving the room. As the door closed, I was surprised to turn to her and see that she had an unpleasant scowl on her face, and a sternness about her demeanor that I knew it was not going to be a conversation about care and concern. To this day, I can still even remember what I was wearing! Talk about the impact this particular teacher had on me! Her face, body language, attitude, and tone somewhat frightened me. Whereas most of my times as a victim were by people who appeared nice enough, she did not appear nice, and that scared me.

When I followed my teacher outside onto the ramp I had no idea what to expect. As soon as the door closed, she started in badgering me. No doubt she was loud enough that at least two or three of the other classrooms full of students could hear since we were a ramp school with open hallways. "You should be ashamed of the way you dress! I've watched you to see if you would correct the problem or not, but you just seem to enjoy being defiant of the school's dress code," she blaringly said. Since I knew I had somewhat been hiding in my clothes for the past few months (especially since the p.e. weight chart), I really wasn't sure what she was talking about. I sat there slack jawed, getting more scared by the minute, as she seemed to step closer and closer with each word. "It is important that we are all aware of ourselves and how we present ourselves to others. You are smart enough to see yourself and be aware of yourself. The way you dress for a young lady your size is completely inappropriate," she continued. Immediately I felt the redness creep into my face as I looked down at my purple and white stripped sweater and stretchable stirrup pants. Yes, they were tighter than I would've preferred but they were stretchy pants, and that was all I could fit into. Here I had initially been hopeful that a teacher was opening a doorway for my screams to be heard, only to feel like she had slammed it right in my face. I was still passed by and falling through the cracks, but now I was just being reminded of how fat I was on my way down. Still, no one bothered to ever ask any questions. All she had to do was ask why I wore those type of pants, and I would've embarrassingly explained that it was because I had a hard time finding any other pants that fit. I'm sure she could've at least been more tactful, if not helpful. That day was the first time I ever tried bulimia.

My curiosities began very early when I participated on the swim team. I started swimming competitively in elementary school, and turned out to have a natural talent for it. My mom had to work late in the evenings sometimes, so it was arranged that my female swim coach could pick me up from daycare and take me to the pool for swim team practice. I loved our drives there because I could pepper her with as many questions as I wanted, and she never denied me any answers. She had streaks of pink hair and probably a dozen piercings and tattoos. I knew I wanted to be just like her, so I wanted to know every dirty thing that I could find out. Needless to say, once again, I learned a lot and much more than I should've.

At swim team practice, I was always the last one out of the girl's restroom, just in case I could get a glimpse of breasts that were larger than mine, since I was still so young and very small-chested. I would linger to see who had started growing pubic hair and who hadn't, desperately waiting until my body would appear more woman-like. I couldn't even wait until I started my period. I loved the boys uniforms too. So closely showing the difference in their sizes. So easily exposing their length and the beauty of it all. When I swam my laps, goggles tightly strapped to my head, I would always try to sneak a quick glimpse of their smooth bodies and tightly uniformed crotch area. I loved being able to see the distinction of their penis and their balls. I just loved the near nakedness, but then again, it was just one more chance to notice that I needed help, but again I was passed by and good enough at my own game to hide the red flags.

Even in high school, my issues were brought to the direct attention of the guidance counselor, but he assumed that he knew me well enough to know that I wouldn't do such things, and automatically brushed it off. Even though it was my best friend who approached him about me abusing way too many drugs, he didn't even consider the notion twice. He never called me out of class to talk about it and he never contacted my parents. He made a joke about it in later years, as if it was something that was impossible.

Instead of asking a thirteen-year-old suicidal girl why she brought a knife to school, just expel her no questions asked. Isn't that the policy? After years of falling through the cracks and being passed by, that's what it led to.

Memorable Moments

I was one of those kids who was fortunate enough to have both sets of my grandparents and great-grandmothers living within the same town. I visited both of their houses regularly, and my grandmas were like my second mothers. My grandparents, on my father's side of the family, were very special people to me too.

My grandparents were always infamous for going overboard on every fun occasion possible. Easter, Christmas, Thanksgiving, everything that lent itself to a celebration was always a huge event at their house. At Easter, the Easter Bunny always left the biggest baskets possible, and hid nearly five hundred eggs. Now I don't mean this was for the typical children's Easter Egg Hunt, this was for everyone. Aunts, uncles, cousins, my grandparents, and my dad all ran and scattered as fast as my brother did in the race and chase to find as many eggs as possible. Of course, the adults did it fairly so that my brother and I always got the most eggs, but it was always an enormous celebration and cause for rejoicing.

Thanksgiving was celebrated the same way: huge. Grandma would spend days cooking in her tiny sweltering kitchen while my brother and I played with toys, did puzzles, and had our hand lightly swatted a few times for dipping our dirty fingers into her delicious meal items. We watched the parade, eagerly shouting for grandma to "look and see that one" at each and every float as it passed by. She even made food and snacks for our parade watching tradition with the family! What we really wanted was to hurry up and finish the meal itself because every year after the Thanksgiving meal, fun, and laughter, we put up and decorated the first of three Christmas trees!

Stop! No! I Don't Want To! ... Please?

Rumpled sheets,
and whispered cries
He never cared
about the tears in my eyes
One strong thrust,
and a jolt like a knife.
The moment of innocence
was drained from her life.
When it was all over
her spirit had died
She was no longer a child,
but a life without pride.
No more carefree parties
with spin the night friends.
Her world as a child
had come to an end.
No more girl scouts
or Barbie doll games.
No more cartoons
because her whole world had changed.
No more dreams
for the life that she led.
Despite all her efforts
she just longed to be dead.

Age 13 before admitting the rape to anyone

CHAPTER 8

It Is All My Fault!

The man who raped me doesn't even deserve a fictitious name in my life so I'll just refer to him as the Jerk. I had not always known the Jerk, as I was eight years younger than him. It all started when I dated a kind-hearted, yet wanting to be mischievous boyfriend, Andrew. I was barely thirteen and Andrew was a lifeguard, and was cute. It was a warm summer before my eighth grade year, and I was excited about being in the oldest grade at school. He was fifteen, and romance was in the air. We met at the beach site where he worked. I think I came on to him more than he did to me. Considering girls generally mature faster than boys, and the fact that I was darkly more matured that most people, we weren't on the same level. He was more interested in video games than girls. Although we never even kissed, we did hang out on occasion so I met a few of his friends. Since he was in high school some of his friends were even older than he was, I *felt* older, and decided I was old enough to fit in to the older crowd. His oldest friend was sixteen. I was thirteen, but it was so cool that older guys were impressed by me and wanted to be with me.

It didn't take much to stay within the loop of their friends since friendships often spread. I certainly was precocious and somewhat attractive, and even more willing to be mischievous and promiscuous. Andrew's friends became my new best friends and the older, the better. Even after Andrew and I broke up very sweetly and innocently, I still stayed in close contact with his friends. I think I always felt drawn to them because they were "the bad boys," and they made me feel like a sexy woman. I knew they were trouble makers in school, even though we attended different schools. Despite the differences in what grade we were in, we still talked about school so I learned about how much fun they had getting in trouble. They were fun, and I felt GOOD acting older. Through Andrew's original friends, I had made other friends. I loved it! A bunch of much older high school students, and even men! WOW! They enjoyed being with me, liked me, and thought I was sexy! That's how I met the Jerk. I always talked and visited all the other guys just as frequently as I could, but since the Jerk was the oldest at twenty-one, he didn't have the restrictions of school, homework, and parents like the rest of us did. He just happened to be able to be around me much more often.

Part of me knew we weren't "boyfriend and girlfriend" but I certainly wanted to be, and part of me actually believed that we were. I was to embarrassed and inexperienced to ever say it to him, but I wanted that kind of relationship so it seemed only natural when we started fooling around. My bipolar disorder was all over the place over it all. One moment I would feel like we were truly in love, and another moment I would be suicidal thinking that he didn't love me as much as I thought he did. I was very inexperienced. Up to this point all I had done was French kiss a boy in kindergarten and kiss a boy in sixth grade once – no tongue even! I had no experience, was scared about learning, wanted to please the Jerk sexually within my limits, and had fun learning. He taught me everything - for the obvious reasons of course – no strings attached! It was simple, my mom would take a shower at night and I would slip out of bed and disengage the house alarm. When he got off work he would knock on my window to wake me up. I'd sleepily meet him in the backyard where we would fool around. My mom never knew any better because the house alarm never went off, as I had sneakily turned it off earlier. I was thirteen, had just started the beginning of my eighth grade school year, and had never done anything sexual. He sure had a great time teaching me though, however much my poor choices in allowing it would later affect me.

Until my eighth grade year, I had actually cared enough about my disguises that I keep my grades up so that no one would look at me any more closely. I practiced piano and thrived at my lessons. I went to swim team practice daily, and continued to be one of the best swimmers in the area. I played at recitals and curtseyed when the audience members clapped. I competed in some of the biggest swimming competitions in our state, and swam that much faster, pushed by the adrenaline of the crowd. As long as I had good grades and performances, everyone could still easily think that everything was okay. Obviously I was entranced by all the things I was doing wrong though. For the first time, once I let go of caring and hope I almost felt *right*. I could live bipolar and borderline, and no one could be disappointed in me if I just lowered the standards of their expectations of me. I had deep and scary problems before I was raped, but I actually cared somewhat about trying to cover up my inner bipolar turmoil. After I was raped, the biggest change in me was that I didn't care about any disguises anymore. I gave up trying to convince myself and others that I wasn't darkly disturbed. I let go and gave up.

Before the rape I skipped school once and invited the Jerk over so that we could fool around. I was so nervous that morning, complaining to my mom that I didn't feel well. She didn't believe me, but I was more upset about the possibility of missing him than I was worried about getting in trouble with the school or my mom. I called the school myself and acted to be my mom claiming that I would be out sick that day. I was so nervous, but tremendously excited at the same time. I tried to dress as sexy as possible, and was thrilled to lead the fun with the Jerk to the bedroom. Remember, most of the time we had to fool around in the backyard because it was late at night when my mom was home and I was supposed to be sleeping. I couldn't very well fool around in my room and risk being caught during those nights! We fooled around for quite a while. Again, I loved all the feelings he was able to pleasure me with, and I loved being able to give him pleasure although he did always get a little rough. I just thought that was how it was supposed to be, and never complained. It wasn't like he was asking for sex or anything, so what did it matter if some of the other things we did hurt a little, I thought. For several hours that day we fooled around. He did ask for sex, whereas he hadn't previously, but he didn't pressure me. When he was ready to leave, he left.

I cannot remember how long this relationship lasted, but it seemed like an eternity to me. In all probability, it was probably only about a month. Sometimes he and I spent time together in the backyard alone, and whenever he had some of our mutual friends with him, we kept "us" a secret. We would all go together to a late night diner, skinny dipping, joy riding, or anything else that gave up any excuse for mischief. It didn't matter because I was a grown up doing grown up things! Of course I wasn't mature enough to realize that the reason he kept our relationship secret is because he knew how wrong it was. He knew from the beginning how wrong it was to be doing the things he was with me. I don't know if he was afraid one of the other guys would tell me that he didn't really care about me, or if he was afraid of the legal ramifications. Either way, when we were around our mutual friends though, he and I kept our outside activities private and personal.

Finally, the night of September 30th. The night started off as common as the other nights. The Jerk had to work late, he always did, so it was no surprise that he didn't knock on my window until about two in the morning. That was our routine. He would knock on my bedroom window to wake me up and I'd meet him in the backyard and perform sexual favors for him until he wanted to leave, basically. I didn't mind though. One part of my personality thought it was a real relationship. This time I let him sneak in my bedroom though since he claimed to need to lay down after work this time because he was more tired than usual. Not to mention, it was raining outside too. Once quietly settled in my room, we started fooling around as usual. I could taste the alcohol on his breath, but it was fun being so grown up and sneaky too. Again the warmth of his fingers, the throbbing of his penis, the forced soreness he caused in my throat. I easily allowed it though considering I thought that was how it was supposed to be. What started off innocently enough didn't take long before I reached the moment that would change my life forever.

Rarely did we both ever get completely naked because it was too uncomfortable in the back yard, but on occasion we did. Suddenly this time was different because we were *inside* and he was getting totally naked. I wasn't sure what else to do, so I willingly did too. NEVER before had he put his penis near my vagina so I wasn't the least bit worried. We fooled around as we always did and he performed oral sex on me for the first time. Then he started asking about having sex, as I felt his hard penis pushing against my leg as he leaned back. I said no easily and comfortably. This time he persisted more with his pleas as he moved his penis up between my legs. I started clenching my legs together at the knees, but when he forcefully pushed them apart, I knew there was nothing "usual" about being with him this time. "I don't want to have sex," I said, just in case he had misunderstood.

"I can't", I said. I felt the slight wetness his tip as he pressed his way closer to me. Immediately I was scared. I wasn't scared that he was going to rape me, but no matter how much I fantasized about sex, I was still young enough to be scared of it. "Please can we?" he begged. "I just can't," I said. "I'm sorry, but I just cant. I don't feel ready. Maybe one day though, so please don't be mad at me." Here I was rambling and apologizing like crazy, and he was mentally preparing to rape me. He pushed against me again, "it won't hurt and I'll be careful." If you really loved me, you would. I'll even wear a condom if you want," he said as he started piercing my insides. "No!" I said more firmly. I didn't want to. Plain as that. I just didn't want to.

Finally, he got tired of my begging not to, apologies, resists, and excuses, and shoved himself into me as hard as he could again and again, faster and faster, harder and harder. I yelped with pain, and he didn't miss a beat. He harshly clasped his hand over my mouth, and whispered in my ear "shut the fuck up, or I will hurt you and your family because you are causing them so much trouble!" Thrust, pain, thrust, pain, then the tears came as I finally gave up. It hurt so bad. Not at all like I fantasized losing my virginity, making love, or sex to be. He pushed himself so hard and far into me that I thought it was going to crush my insides. I envisioned a knife finally piercing my heart because my body was now as broken and damaged as my mind and soul already were. I cried and moaned "no" the whole time. The physical pain was like an explosion from the inside. He rammed, crushed, and drove himself into me; regardless of my anguish.

Condom or not, he didn't care. Even though it only lasted a few sweaty minutes before he climbed off, as the stickiness of his cum covered me and my blanket that I slept with every night, I knew that I would never be the same and just prayed that he would leave me; naked and alone. And believe it or not, after all that, he was pissed because he couldn't find his contact lens. I didn't care what I had to do to get this man out of my house and life, so I quickly helped him find it, and locked the door behind him after he casually left. I never expected an apology, but he sauntered off and didn't even look back. He had shattered my innocence, and didn't even feel guilty enough to look back at the home and the family of people he had destroyed.

I don't know if the Jerk always planned to rape me, or if the fooling around just gave him the perfect excuse he had been waiting on. I'll never know, and it wouldn't make a difference anyways. He was someone I foolishly considered a friend, and regardless of his reason, he raped me. I never slept that night. I couldn't bring myself to clean myself or my sheets up either. All I could do was curl up in a ball, and cry. I cried because I knew that I had always been different from other children. I cried because I missed my grandma, who had recently passed away. I cried because I didn't even fit in with the friends I use to have who were the same age as me. I cried because I couldn't keep up the disguise no matter how hard I tried. I cried because I couldn't get the time and things I needed to just go ahead and kill myself. Finally, I let go, and felt the gut wrenching sobs because I had been raped, violated to the heart and soul, and destroyed.

The next morning, I covered the evidence by hiding the blood spattered sheets in my closet and throwing away the pajamas I had worn the night before. I went to school. I went to class. I spoke when spoken to. Life went on as normal as I could make it appear. Even though I had been raped only days before, I squealed with all the other teenagers at the pep rally. I was manic by then, and tried not to think about the rape. I colored blue ink colored hearts on the inside of my locker with a football player's number. I excitedly went to the football game, spilled popcorn at every one of our team's touchdowns as we leaped to cheer for our team, and danced to every song our band played. That's the great thing about being manic. You are so happy that you don't care about anything but the glory you are feeling.

It would only be days later that I began self-mutilating, and calling my mother to say my final goodbye. Bipolar crash! The other side of borderline. Aside from mental illness or not, I let go and gave up. I couldn't handle the reality of what had just happened to me, and I couldn't handle the low that came with bipolar and major mood depressive disorder. I cheered at a football game and pep rally, squealed about boys, gossiped with other girls, gave up, tried to kill myself, and was hospitalized – all within a week, but that's bipolar touched by borderline for you. You never know how or when, how short or how long, and when (if ever) it's going to end.

My first outlet for my pain was like the first time you use a drug. No matter how many times or how much you do it later, you never quite reach the high of your first time. My cure was a magical cure! Cutting! Self-mutilation! What a miraculous temporary fix it offered. I do not have any idea what gave me the idea, but after that first cut, I was hooked just as I would've been if it was a drug. It was my drug! It was my self-medicating relief! Slicing, watching skin splitting, feeling blood droplets forming and running like rain down your skin…it became my sensory cure, but the euphoric feelings never lasted long. What was my solution to continuing to feel better? Continue cutting! Deeper, more frequently, in safe unseen areas so as not to be noticed, and in dangerous areas when I was practicing for my final departure. I already knew one day I was going to kill myself, but for right now, "don't let go…yet" and cutting was enough to make it through one more day.

I still vividly remember my first cut. It was on my ankle in the shape of a heart. I specifically pierced the middle of a heart with an arrow through it because in my darkly twisted mind, this represented my damaged, irreparable, sinful heart, mind, body, and soul. I didn't do it like other typical preteens and teenagers do when they doodle hearts and arrows on their notebooks. Typical girls that age draw hearts and arrows to represent love, boyfriends, girlfriends, crushes, etc. I did it sharply, slicing skin, and not representative at all of what other teenage girls were thinking when they drew their hearts and arrows. I did it to represent how damaged and broken my heart was, and how it had been destroyed beyond repair or stitching. I started with a protractor, but couldn't get it to cut as sharply and accurately as

I wanted. I searched the cabinet drawers for the perfect knife. Nothing! Finally I found the perfect knife. Small, easy to hold and maneuver, already I was feeling even more excited about my project.

My first cut, my heart, also probably took the longest because I savored the sensation of every cut more since it was so new to me. I would slice a curve of the heart, and sit and watch mesmerized as the skin split and blood droplets formed. I would retrace the pattern with the knife again, ensuring a deep enough slit to make my skin art (and for another enlightening feeling at the deeper pain). It felt like I glowed with warmth as the blood started running down the side of my ankle. I started the point where the two curves of a heart meet, and carefully snagged at the skin to make the perfect shape. It was my pain relief, it was my art, it was my spirit. It was an expression of how badly I was hurting. I just didn't know it at the time. Only the first few times, and special times, did I actually cut that specifically. Most of the time I just cut however quickly, angrily, and conveniently I could, without any attention to detail or body placement. This time was different though because it marked the beginning of a new addiction and an even more serious problem.

The more I cut, the more skillful I became at it. It was my art, and my sense of expression. I liked being able to control my pain, because in essence, that's what it felt like I was doing. Initially I started with any sharp object I could find; protractor, needles, the obvious – knives, shards of broken glass, anything! I loved the "fix" of it. I looked forward to it. In one of my lowest bipolar lows, I even carved the word DIE into my ankle. Along with several others, it is a self-inflicted wound that remains a visible scar today; visible evidence of the journey I had to endure to reach my new beginning. While other preteens and teenagers in class distractedly thought about dating, television, music, and video games, I was daydreaming about how and when I would perform a new cut. It felt as sweet to me as music does to the ears, heart, and soul.

Finally, it did become a hard, real, true addiction. I couldn't *not* cut. I had to! I NEEDED to! A quick solid slice before I took a shower before going to school. A razor blade hidden in my pocket at school for a quick cut or two if I timed it right during the day. That meant leaving one class a minute or two early because "it was a bathroom emergency", as I claimed to the teacher. I would take my backpack along since the bell would be ringing soon, and would have at least seven minutes to cut if I stuck to my routine. Leave one class early, and go to the next class the last second that the bell rang. That gave me enough time to slice, feel the dripping blood in all its glory, watch as the skin stretched even further (as I had progressed to rapid, thrusting cuts deeper than when I first started), quickly apply a band-aid, and then make it to the next class without anyone being suspicious.

I was in a tremendous bipolar low that had begun sinking even further. Of course this was also due to Post Traumatic Stress Disorder as a result of the rape that I refused to admit to anyone, but the bipolar low didn't make matters any easier. I couldn't get out of the low. I didn't want to get out of it either because I didn't care. I didn't even care if anyone even noticed or not, at that point. I wanted to cut so the bad blood could escape. I wanted to binge and purge myself of my inner evils by cutting. I binged and purged, literally as I had been dabbling with eating disorders since the sixth grade p.e. and clothing talk incidents. I wanted to appear beautiful since I couldn't at least be normal, so I wanted to go forever without eating. I hadn't yet gotten to drugs, although I had been drinking with my guy friends for a while. I didn't want anyone to notice, but I didn't exactly care enough about myself to care if anyone did notice. But someone did notice. Mom. I hated her for it though. Who the hell did she think she was taking my safely collected stash of sharpened objects, hiding the sharpest objects in the house, warning school counselors? Screw her, I thought. I'll find a way to cut when and where I want to regardless! Now though, I have to admit, way to go mom!

At first the school therapist jokingly worked with me. This only lasted for about two or three weeks, but it is almost laughingly funny. She was so uncaring, and so tied up with her other arrangements that I know the only reason she met with me was basically to call my mom and tell her I was "doing fine." The counselor just wanted to cover her own ass by following through on the request of a parent. I'm not even sure the counselor remembered my name without looking at my file as I sat right there in front of her. She never asked how I felt. She never offered solutions. She never gave me statistics about how many middle students feel the same way that I did. She didn't try to talk about sex, drugs, or peer pressure. She basically called me out of class for twenty minutes every other day or so and read a few of my poems. What did I care? It was getting my out of class! She would read a poem or two (of course some of the happier ones I wrote when I was in mania) and praise me for my writing. Case closed. I would get a pass back to class, and be deemed "normal" once again.

Throughout my entire cutting experience I was in therapy. My grandmother had died a few months earlier, and I had been demonstrating some "depression-like" behaviors, so my parents already had me in therapy. I liked the woman too. She was easy to talk to, smoked (which made me comfortable because my grandmother had too), and it seemed like she really cared. I liked her for that. I couldn't even see what the real problem was. So what that I was incredibly way too sexually promiscuous? So what that I was giving sexual invitations to older teenage men, even though I was only twelve and thirteen at the time? They liked me, so why not continue to be flirty and cute,… and maybe even lose my virginity before I make my final cut? Why not sneak away every now and then to get naked with a boy much older than me? Virgin or not, I loved being able to be so close to something so inappropriate and dangerous, yet so appealing. What was the problem with any of it?

I still wasn't going to tell my therapist about my cutting though. Even I knew better than that. I knew she wouldn't understand it. We had worked well together since I had started seeing her, but I hadn't progressed. We had talked a lot about my family, my grandmother, my recent actions and wants involving older men, and a wide array of other topics; except, for the actual truth. As the bipolar raged within me, I was nearly ready to implode from within. The borderline was finally becoming too much to handle and cover up. I was a time bomb ticking way too quickly, and just waiting to explode. I talked openly about the things my therapist had on our agenda to discuss, but I didn't tell her the truth unless she asked. Most of the time, either personality could answer with an honest answer without letting on about how screwed up I really was because she didn't exactly pinpoint the questions exactly right. She was still getting to know me, so it wasn't as if she didn't try to help. She was just having to take a lot of notes and spend time getting to know me verses the troubled me.

Finally the school caught on, but being the geniuses they were, they just chose to send the problem away rather than take a closer look. The only way they even became aware of a problem is because my mom had to call and tell *them*! I had finally picked the perfect day for my suicide. I hadn't planned it that way, but it was too beautiful of a day for me to enjoy it any other way. I had the perfectly selected knife, studded blade so that it would tear at the flesh more raggedly doing a better job severing veins, tucked safely in my backpack. I didn't want to do it that morning though because I did want to spend my last day eating a nice lunch with my few friends at school, gossiping for the last time about newly developed and broken up couples. That was my final goodbye with them, not that I was going to tell them that. I just wanted to see them once more. I just wanted to soak it all in before leaving for good.

My plan was simple really. I was going to walk to school, as I usually did, spend half of the day safely at school in my classes, have lunch with my friends, and skip the afternoon of school to discretely go off forever by myself. Even though I had decided that morning that I was going to kill myself, I hadn't necessarily planned it that day, so I did legitimately feel like I wanted to say goodbye in some small ways. I thought it would all go over so easily that I wouldn't have any problems.

On my way to school, I felt that it only appropriate to tell my mom that I loved her, thank her, and tell her that it wasn't her fault. Of course I didn't come right out and tell her that I was going to kill myself that day, but I did just want to take the time to reassure her how much I loved her. I didn't have to say it though because my mom heard it in my voice and felt my pain in her heart. My plan was that I'd kill myself before I talked to her again, and just writing it in a letter seemed to impersonal. I called her on the way to school, as was our normal routine anyways, to say my final goodbye. It wasn't that I didn't love her or anyone else enough to continue living, I just couldn't handle living within myself let alone love myself enough not to commit suicide. I was too young, and hadn't thought far ahead enough in my plans to realize that she would obviously try to get help and call the school. Immediately she called for help, and I was never able to follow through with my plans. As soon as I arrived at the school, they searched my things, found my weapon, and decided to make an example out of me that sent the message that threats and weapons would not be tolerated. My mom had clearly told them that I was going to kill myself, but the school broadcast it as a troubled girl who was going to try to harm or kill others. I was immediately expelled, no questions asked. That's the policy.

Throughout all my cutting, not only did it help me find a temporary fix, but it also helped me form a suicide plan more clearly, and I knew with renewed excitement and reassurance that it would work. Since my previous attempt had been faltered,

I was ecstatic! One week later, I eagerly told my therapist about my suicide plan (since she was my only friend or attachment after being expelled). I was manic, and I couldn't wait to share with a special friend my magnificent plan. That was the day I entered and became a resident at hospital number one. We'll call it Death's Doorway (obviously, not it's real name, but even as an adult, my opinion is that it should be!).

Memorable Moments

One special time that my dad and I had together was our trip to the Miss Teen Pageant. I don't want to brag, but I did mention that during my high school years I broke away from my ugly duckling shell and became the beautiful swan (on the outside, anyways). I was selected to represent Miss Teen for our area and compete at the state level for the title for our state. Dad and I went together and had a better time than any of the other girls with moms who were fixated on their daughters looking perfect.

We decided that since we were there, why not make a vacation out of it too? We went to Disney, King Author's Feast, and as many other fun places as we could squeeze around pageant times and performances. Hours and hours of time were spent towards perfecting the dance that was choreographed for all of us. We rehearsed our order and line up for entrance. We practiced gliding in high heels instead of fumbling with two left feet. The best moments I had though was when my dad was near my side. What a funny pair we made! A roomful of nervous mothers and daughters, and my dad and I just being there for the fun of making it that far to begin with. We were thrilled just to be there: me and dad. Not to say that my focus and seriousness about the pagent wasn't the same, and likewise with my dad as he sat in the front row of the pageant. We just figured that win or lose, let's enjoy the precious time we have together, and we did! To this day, we joke about my dad helping me curl my hair with my treasured curlers and curling iron before the pageant when he didn't even know what a pony tail holder was. We had so many laughs from the experiences, and it was one of the best times we had together. I didn't win the title, but I definitely won in the long run. I had gotten to spend time with the man of my life; my daddy.

I Cried When You Left

You said goodbye.
You walked away.
You gave me a kiss.
But you couldn't stay.
You left without warning.
You left my to cry.
You gave me a hug
and then said goodbye.
You walked down the hall
and turned a corner or two.
You walked through the doors
and I knew that's when I lost you.

Age 13

CHAPTER 8

Death's Doorway: We Can Help (But Don't)

*M*ental health is an area of medicine where great strides have been made and are currently being made. In the time I was demonstrating my array of behaviors not as much was known about mental health, in general, let alone what would eventually become my diagnoses. I saw my therapist, at first, only as needed on a weekly or biweekly schedule. My mom had decided earlier in the summer that I should go to therapy and even though I wasn't thrilled, I wasn't opposed to it either. My moods with everyone always fluctuated: Bipolar! Borderline personality disorder! Sometimes I was happy and eager to see my therapist, excitedly and animatedly talking about my current life. Other times I was sullen, discussed self destructive impulses and behaviors, how much I hated *everything*, and how much I just wanted to curl up and die.

Although I wasn't happy going to therapy over the summer, it was definitely the right thing for my mom to insist since I had drastically gone downhill since my grandmother passed away. I loved being out of school because it meant I could take every sneaky opportunity possible to do something I considered great, but knew that others would reprimand me for. I just couldn't live the way I was supposed to. I just didn't feel that way. Nothing inside me had ever worked that way. The summer marked the beginning of my nights sneaking out, so it was only a matter of time before I crashed and burned. Bipolar disorder insanity practically! I instantly fell in love with sneaking out. I loved taking risks with people, sometimes people I barely even knew. I loved being so secretive, so bold and brave, so open minded to any trouble that would come our way. These were the first times I tried drinking and smoking – I was such a grown up! In other words, the things I was doing would've gotten much worse and more dangerous and deadly before they got better if my mom hadn't made the decision she made at the time.

Mental inpatient care can be received either willingly or unwillingly, if any of two specific indicators are present; if you have a plan to kill yourself, or if you have a plan to kill someone else. In either case, inpatient treatment is mandatory. It is also mandatory under other specific scenarios, but any response that indicates yes to the two indicators is a guarantee to impatient treatment. Impatient care is also recommended if an individual with a mental illness has needs that *need* to be met that day, even if it is as simple as the need for an easy medication adjustment or refill, or phone call returned by your Doctor. Willing admittance means that you, of your own consent, agree to be admitted to a facility. In the case that you refuse admission, it is only a matter of minutes before a judge can order a Baker Act: meaning that you are court ordered and admitted against your will. What choice did I have? Either way, the end result would've been the same.

The day I was expelled for taking a knife to school, my mom had me in the therapist's office as an emergency appointment.

When we left my therapists office, my mom drove me directly to the hospital. I didn't have anything specific on my mind, except that this was going to be a few days away from the mother I thought I hated. I figured it would be a few days, and not too bad…besides, it's not like you ever heard stories of anyone going to a place like this during this time and at my age. If anything, I was frustrated because I knew it would keep me away from my guy friends for a few days, and that part I hated! I think my mom was afraid I would try to run away if we came home to collect a few of my belongings first. All I had was the actual clothes that I was wearing; half of which ended up being contraband, according to their dress code policy. I didn't know that it was going to be so horrible, otherwise I would've thought up every idea I could in order to try to run away. I didn't really know what to expect. To a thirteen year old, the word "hospital" did not imply the experiences I would have when I became a patient though.

Hours and hours it seemed, I sat in the waiting room absent mindedly thumbing through the pages of boring adult magazines. My mom was in an office with the doors closed (one of those with a window so that we could still see each other). Every now and then I caught a sympathetic glimpse from her and a stern look from the woman she was talking to. I still had no idea what was going on or what was being discussed. I wasn't interested in knowing. I knew I was going to a "special hospital" but I had no idea what that meant. I noticed a phone on the wall beside the office my mom was in. I took it as an opportunity to call my friends and complain. I only called a few people, but they didn't seem surprised. It wasn't even worth the effort of the call then in my opinion.

In the time that I was waiting I had plenty of time to think. I thought about how much I missed my grandmother, how disappointed my family would be when my mom told them I was here, and how much I just wished I could be normal. I thought about how the art I had been creating lately was beautiful, however deathly morbid it may have been. I thought about my poems, how they bared my soul, which obviously ached to be eliminated. I thought about how I wound up here, but couldn't come up with a definitive answer. Obviously it was because I was going to kill myself, but how did it go this far? I couldn't figure that out because it felt like I had just always been this way. Of course I knew some of the actions were wrong, but I sincerely didn't know it was wrong to feel the way I felt. I thought about too much.

Finally the door opened and I was beckoned in. "Its about time! You grown ups don't know me, so why should you talk about me like you do?," I thought. The woman introduced herself, but honestly I have no idea what her name was. I didn't really care anyways. I didn't know it at the time, but that was the only time I would see anyone in the front office or even be allowed in the front waiting room, so it didn't really matter if I remembered any of their names or not. In the waiting area and at the reception desk there were vases with fake flowers, magazines, smiling faces, friendly greeters, and pleasant enough looking staff. There wasn't anything out of the ordinary or alarming, except that I did notice a few of this particular woman's frowns from watching her through the door. She explained that I would have to take a few tests, and made me hug and kiss my mom goodbye as we headed to a separate room. "No big deal," I thought. I had seen these types of test before; rate on a scale of one to ten, fill in the bubble, etc. "Bye mom, I'll see you when I finish my tests," I thought.

I don't remember many of the test questions, but I do remember that I circled enough bubbles and scaled enough one to ten answers that I already knew that I was crazy. I was truthful on my tests. Had I known that I was going to be locked away in Death's Doorway for so long, I damn sure wouldn't have been, even though I'll admit that is immature logic. I was smart enough to know the possible consequences of some of the tests, but I had also known for a long time that something was wrong with me. If I could get those answers from the tests, I *wanted* to be as honest as possible. I actually just wanted to die! If I couldn't, fine, I would accept the help as long as it didn't keep making me feel as shitty as I had been for a long time now. I would be happy at the help, as long as it didn't *hurt* me more than it *helped* me. Unfortunately, it hurt me on so many more levels than it helped.

Once the tests were completed and reviewed it confirmed what I already felt, but in fewer words. I was crazy, damaged, screwed up, fucked up, and didn't stand a chance! I actually do not know or remember what the tests indicated, but I was started on a large medication regiment the next day, so I can only assume it had to do with the test results. Since I was so young the doctors talked to my mom about the results more than they did me, so I really had no idea what I was being treated for most of the time. I was admitted as an acute – short term - care patient (A.T.C for acute treatment care) and locked on a unit where I was the youngest patient. The oldest patient was seventeen, but I was easily the youngest. I was scared already, and my mom probably hadn't even made it out of the parking lot. I hadn't even completely realized that I'd have to leave my mom who I seemed to both love and hate.

I can imagine her sobbing at the steering wheel before even attempting to start the car because I know it must have been as hard for her to leave me, as it was for me to have to stay there. I still didn't know what was in store for me, but I would soon find out that it was not anything helpful or good. Then again, I'll admit that part of that was my fault and due to my suffering from mental illness undiagnosed and incorrectly medicated. I could've made the experience there more helpful if I had tried with the right supports. Hours later my mom returned with items I would want and need, but they wouldn't even let me see her again. Too untheraputic, I'm sure – what harm could it have caused? I was thirteen, damaged, broken, and scared! As typical with my bipolar disorder, I was both excited and terrified. I was manic about doing something new that would obviously get me attention, and I felt depressed because I knew deep down that I really needed the attention and help, but still wouldn't be able to be fixed.

Memorable Moments

At my grandma and grandpa's on my father's side of the family we always had our special Christmas traditions. Long before Christmas Even we would help put up a total of three Christmas trees. Grandma always had the artificial tree in the living room, and two real ones in the family room. Now the two real Christmas trees weren't just any trees. One was always astronomical in size! Grandma always bought her trees from the same seller, so intentionally, they would hold back the biggest one for her every year. The second one of course had to be smaller, but if your going to have two, you might as well have three, right? Grandma loved Christmas! She lived for it (and for her grandchildren)! She would read our favorite Christmas books a million times in the month of December. She would play the more advanced Christmas piano songs that I loved but couldn't quite play. She would teach me so many Christmas songs on the piano that I must have driven her crazy with my hunting and pecking to try to find the right keys, but she always praised me on how well I did. After out Christmas Eve meal, it was nearly torture for my brother and me! We were allowed to open five or six presents, but we had to wait until the dishes were picked up and cleaned. Torture! The wait seemed to last forever! It was this way for everyone. We all opened a few presents. It would only be Christmas Eve, and the room always looked like the Christmas tornado had roared through already.

The memories of the Christmas I spent there are so powerful and special that they represent everything that I want to be able to do for my children. It was perfect. Not because of all the presents and excitement, but because we all felt so loved. My brother and I smiled through the hundreds of pictures that were taken and we hopped from lap to lap to show off our newly opened treasures. That first step into the room Christmas morning always moved me beyond words. The room would always be filled from wall to wall with presents and gifts from Santa. Now, my grandparents didn't necessarily buy the most expensive presents in the world, but somehow it was always exactly what we wanted.

The Rose of Death

A day with sea breeze blowing.
No regret or loss is showing.
My feelings growing deep,
as water wades across my feet.
The cries of seabirds in the sky,
questions time of death – just why?
A silver blade upon my wrist.
My tears so hot they are a mist.
A pistol cocked upon my head.
I'm wishing now that I were dead.
A rope and rose tied at my neck.
Deeply thorns tear at my flesh.
Dead mans float upon the sea,
questioning, could this be me?
I toss the pills deep down my throat.
Death Keeper brings to me a boat.
I flip the switch and walk the dunes.
My nightfall will be coming soon.
My life is coming to an end.
I'm lost alone, without a friend.
The waves are crashing on the shore,
and soon I will be – nevermore.

Age 14

CHAPTER 9

Sorry Folks, I Cant Be Treated!

I was admitted to the hospital on October 6th in the A.T.C. facility (acute treatment care) and moved to the R.T.C. facility (residential treatment care) on November 5th. After just one month the psychiatrists, therapists, and staff determined that I was so screwed up that it would take longer than a few weeks to fix or teach me. Altogether I spent one month in the acute treatment care facility, and another six months in the residential facility. As with the acute treatment care unit, I was the youngest in the residential treatment care facility. The problem was that I didn't fit in anywhere. A feeling I was used to. I didn't fit in on the children's unit, but as time has taught us all, I certainly didn't belong with seventeen and eighteen year olds either.

My time spent in A.T.C was so short that I only have a few memories of it, except that it was a more freely run unit. Sometimes a patient may only stay for three to five days, and then some would be there for two to four weeks. You just never knew.

You could have one roommate one day, and another stranger as your roommate the next day. Then you had the rest of us, like me. Unfixable. Within a month I had become a residential patient. I was so low and improperly medicated and undiagnosed though that I didn't care. I already had my own repertoire of self-medicating skills but I was eager to learn as many more as I could. I became manic about it almost. I picked up on a few things on the acute treatment care unit. You could madly claw at yourself, scream, cuss out people, throw a "temper tantrum", punch walls, rage, and yell, and most of the time nothing would happen.

Since I didn't know who I was or couldn't even handle being the same person all of the time, I just figured I'd do whatever the hell I wanted as each moment came. Everyday I had looked in the mirror it seemed like I saw a different person. Sometimes every hour of the day I felt like a different person. I just couldn't control who I was and what I felt, and my bipolar roller coaster was always stretching beyond the limits of too high and too low. I figured it would be easiest to just live with the label "bad girl" instead of trying to figure out the root of the problem. That's exactly what I did. I cussed out the nurses, staff, doctors, and therapists. I scratched in obvious places, just to imply, "ha, ha, you can't stop me!" I did whatever I wanted, whenever I wanted, and just screamed "fuck you" when any of the consequences were invoked. I annorexically starved myself and binged and purged once I gave in to food. I just didn't care about anything, least of all, me.

On the other hand, they also had a wide range of consequences to *teach you* if you pushed your limits too far. One possible consequence was the torture chamber (yes, I am referring to the tiny padded and carpeted cells with only a slit of a window). They could also make you take a tranquilizer pill to "help" you with self-control but at that point we liked the pills, so sometimes it was worth "going off" just to get the little pill. The absolute worst consequences were restraints and straitjackets. It was a horrific feeling to be tackled, tied down, and harnessed to a bed.

It was enough to make my insides churn because of the loss of control over myself to the point that I couldn't move at all. It felt like a violation. I felt broken, with my small amount of self-esteem diminishing even further as I had to ask a nurse to hold the tissue while I blew my nose. I understand that there are times that restraints and straitjackets are used to protect patients, but I also saw them overused to control or break down the spirits of far too many people. I was one of those people, and it did further damage my spirit. Not being able to move did prove that I wasn't worth anything because the world wasn't affected regardless of whether I moved or not.

The hospital staff and Doctors knew about my cutting, but they didn't seem overly concerned about it at first. It was just another check in the box – "patient did or didn't exhibit self-injurious behavior today." No one seemed to care or ask why. They just wrote down that I did it. Since they didn't have any sharp objects, I had to watch and learn. I learned that you could do almost as much damage, however not quite as deep, with fingernails. I learned that they didn't check behind your ears, which was a good spot to tear up when in school if I acted as if my hand was resting against my head. I learned that they didn't check the less obvious clothed parts of us; for example, ankles under socks. That was another great place to keep it a secret. Fortunately I was still able to relieve myself to some extent by cutting, without anyone seeming too concerned, or at least at the beginning of my stay. Just as fortunate, I learned how to cut and conceal without their knowing once they pretended to care.

While I was in the hospital I still worked with my therapist and psychiatrist. The "best" child psychiatrist in town came to visit me on the ward one day for our appointment and confidently placed a can on his desk. It was the same size and shape as a soda can, all silver, with a wide orange stripe around it about an inch wide. On the strip it had the letters B.S in black letters stamped onto it. He had me take a seat and gruffly explained that it was his "bullshit repellant," so he didn't want to put up with any of my bullshit. Thanks, Doc! Glad you understand how to help me because I'm going to be coming to you for years begging you for help, trusting you with my life as you alter my medications, and praying that you will help save me from myself.

I was passed from list to list of diagnosis. Initially the diagnosis were more simple but as the months passed, the diagnosis suggestions became much more complex. What started as post traumatic stress disorder, depression, and obsessive compulsive disorder turned into schizophrenia, bipolar (also called manic depressive at the time), psychotic, severely emotionally disturbed, multiple personalities, borderline personality disorder, emotionally handicapped…and anything else they could imagine. Instead of determining a correct diagnosis, they just settled on the reasoning that my problems were due to my being manipulative with extreme attention seeking behaviors. They couldn't figure out what was wrong with me. Whatever it was, I had always known that it was bad and was too afraid to let anyone know how disturbed I had always felt.

I was also still working with my normal therapist, who I liked, but even she had been frustrating me more frequently. Usually I felt like I could connect with her at least on some level, but she just pissed me off at some of the things she said now. She defended my mom! She disagreed with me and said that my relationships and friendships were unhealthy! She lectured me on cutting! What did she really know about any of these things? My mom was wrong for having me locked up! My boyfriend (the rapist!), even though he was twenty-one and I was thirteen really, really loved me and my friends were not the ones to blame just because they did bad things too! I began to feel angry and betrayed! The anger within me rose, and I'm sad to admit that I directed most of it towards my mom. I knew that I was wrong, but I needed someone to blame; someone, who would love me even if I was crazy inside and out. No matter what my mom did with me, she couldn't win though. I loved the control of having the capacity to hurt someone else, and to be able to hate.

Finally, after trying to explain my boyfriend again to my therapist, I finally caved. For months I had been telling myself that he liked me, almost loved me, and really cared about me. I knew logically what a twenty-one year old would want a thirteen year old for but at first I really thought it was different. Sure I did things that could get me in trouble but he was never mean to me, so it had to be safe enough right? I enjoyed being able to please the Jerk sexually without "going all the way," I explained to my therapist. I tried to be adamant with my therapist that he only had the nicest intentions. Here in this seemingly sterile environment though the walls were closing in on me fast, and the truth was about to crack. I had already known the truth, but had hoped it would just disappear if I ignored it.

I tried to hold it together by explaining what seemed like a simple enough story about the relationship I had with the Jerk. I explained to my therapist that it was sprinkling outside, so we had our fourplay into the house quietly and sneakily, instead of the backyard. After all, my mom was asleep in the next room, which only added more excitement to the sexual tension that was clearly building. I loved the way his fingers knew where to fit inside me. I had never done that before with anyone else, so it was a mystical feeling. I loved his mouth over my body. The tingles it gave me were different than anything I had ever felt. I didn't even know what a blow job was prior to meeting the Jerk, but he was happy to direct my head, however uncomfortable it may have been to me. I liked experiencing the things I knew I shouldn't be doing and he was my first for all of it. Even though I always knew that he wasn't really my boyfriend, since those are things you would do with a boyfriend, I had bragged to my therapist that he was. My first boyfriend, at that! It made me feel grown up. I finally described the night of September 30th to her as if the Jerk and I had made love for the first time. Somehow between her caring and empathetic eyes, the sob threatening to escape my throat and the black cloud of truth overshadowing me, I cracked and sold the secrets of my soul; my wrongdoings that caused this to happen. I admitted that I was raped, and that it was all my own fault.

When it all finally came out to the therapist, I remember I was sobbing and screaming by the end of it, "I TRIED TO STOP HIM! I KEPT TELLING HIM NO, BUT HE KEPT PUSHING INSIDE ME! HE SAID I WOULD IF I REALLY LOVED HIM, BUT I BEGGED HIM TO WAIT UNTIL I WAS READY. HE DIDN'T. HE, HE, HE….RAPED ME! I'M ALREADY DEAD INSIDE ANYWAYS, BUT YES, HE…HE… HE… RAPED ME!" Are you finally happy, I thought, now that I admitted what he did? I could barely handle knowing myself, and even thinking or remembering it. I had already scattered the pieces of my life puzzle by falling in love with self mutilating, being admitted to Death's Doorway for the sake of being kept alive due to numerous suicide attempts and plans. Admitting the rape just made the puzzle pieces of my carefully constructed array of disguises burn and dissipate like ashes until there was nothing left of me. I revealed it to the world by telling her, and released a secret I had been trying so hard to forget, ignore, and scare away!

Even though I had only exaggeratedly thought that it meant "revealing it to the world," it actually was revealed to my world. As with any other crime, the police had to investigate. It didn't matter that weeks had passed from the time the Jerk committed the act until I finally admitted it. I still had to relive every single moment in detail with the police, all the while hysterically sobbing and simply missing my mommy. After the police questioned me the same day as I admitted the rape, the investigation was started. It was in the newspaper the very next day. I did have to deal with revealing it to my world after all. And that's not even including the feelings I had as a child gynecologist examined me to confirm that I was not a virgin (as I had already told them – HE RAPED ME!) Didn't they get it?!?! The Jerk raped me and I was destroyed! I didn't need an exam to know how badly I had ruined myself, and a police investigation to prove that it was all my fault.

I still didn't understand though. How could they tell me that the Jerk was wrong to rape me when I said no, and then turn around and make me do something else I didn't want to do such as like spread my legs for a gynecologist to examine me? Why did everyone have such a problem with the word NO? No, I didn't want to have sex with him. No, I didn't want to have to tell anyone. No, I didn't want my disguises to fail. No, I didn't want a Doctor to do a gynecological exam. Regardless of the times I said no though, it never seemed like I was being heard. What defines a good touch and a bad touch, a right or a wrong touch if the exam and their results feel as mortifying as the rape did? I don't know what the police and gynecological doctor expected to find. In some minor way though, it validated that despite my craziness, it had happened. I may have sold my soul and told about the terrible things I had done, but at least it allowed me to set the truth free. I didn't feel any less guilty about causing my own rape, but at least it was one less disguise I would have to keep up by admitting that it wasn't by my choice to have sex. I began to understand for the first time that I had lost my virginity because I had been raped. *I was raped.* Those words hurt my soul, let alone the taste they left in my mouth when I tried to say it. I had known this all along, but was too ashamed, embarrassed, and mentally screwed up about it. I just hadn't known what to do any sooner. I had hoped that I could just forget about it. I had hoped that I would die, so that none of it would matter anyways.

The hospital staff were beginning to get on to me too much about my cutting though since they considered it a sinking sign of post traumatic stress disorder due to the rape, so I had to be careful. I had to find another outlet. I was burning with inner pain, and needed to release it with control over my outside self-inflicted pain. I was desperate! My insides were hurting so bad, that I had to find a way to make the outside pains feel worse. I suddenly crashed again. Welcome again to the world of a bipolar! I grabbed anything I could, the more blunt the better. A can of shaving cream. A thick wooden brush handle. Anything hard that I could find, and I slammed it into my wrist as hard as I could as many times as I could. When my right arm was exhausted from beating my left wrist, I temporarily took a break by just slamming my already damaged wrist into dressers, beds, and any other object I could see that was hard. This went on for hours, until I was finally exhausted enough to sleep. The bipolar in me was manic over it. I know it is hard to believe someone could be so happy beating themselves, but there was something electrifying about watching the swelling, seeing the purplish color of skin darkening, feeling the strain of trying to move my wrist. It was all such a powerful feeling, and the borderline personality only furthered my convictions that I needed to do it to make myself feel better and that it really was okay. Of course it was noticed the next day and I was rushed to the emergency room for x-rays. Believe it or not, it was actually fun being let off the ward, even if it was only to go to another Doctor and admit to him that I was crazy enough to do this to myself. Severe bruising, several fractures, a hard cast later, and I was led back to my room. For the moment, fracturing my wrist was my fix, so it was alright in my world for the time being. As always, only a short time though.

Over stimulating myself with cutting too much would always shoot me strait into mania like a rocket, or to the depths of despair of slicing to kill myself. Just knowing that I could find a way to cut was enough temptation that I couldn't stand NOT cutting. Not even after the shattering of my wrist bones incident. I just *had* to cut! My bipolar needed the high from cutting and my moods would always irrevocably go back and forth, so there was always a constant *need* to cut. I could feel the roller coaster climbing the rails up and I could feel that I was ascending towards mania already. The only way I knew to deal with mania was to cut, so I was scared about how to find to some other way to rid myself of the demons that seemed to control me if I couldn't cut. For days, I avoided cutting in every way I knew. Starvation. I would tease myself by eating at breakfast, and then look forward to the pains I would feel during the day and later that night as my body craved for food. That was only a temporary fix though, because as an accomplished anorexic, my body was still use to going without food when I chose to. Even the combination with bulimia didn't ease my desire to cut any. I would eat a bag of cookies from the vending machine, purge them, and still ache to cut. Finally I just gave up and didn't care if it was a secret anymore or not. I hurt, so what the hell if the whole world knows? Nothing can fix me anyways, so fuck it all! I scratched violently at my arms, my wrists, or any other convenient and easily reachable body part. Knowing the treatment plans they had for me, they probably left the cast on longer intentionally because that gave me one less wrist I couldn't slice. I was always lectured, but never asked why. I don't know if I could've answered that question, but it sure would've been nice if someone has asked, just in case I did have an answer.

I had also easily noticed that I had gained quite a bit of weight since being in the hospital too, so it was easy enough to go back to anorexia, in addition to my perfected bulimic schedule. You may be hungry the first day or two, and even have some headaches, but after that it just feels like your body doesn't need food. The part of you that needs to eat just feels like it dies off. Anorexia and bulimia were just two more ways to kill off just one more part of me; one more piece of my deteriorating puzzle. I loved anorexia! Such control! I loved watching the Doctors and nurses squirm, worried that I wasn't eating. I loved smirking at their scowls when they checked the box on my chart at every meal: refused to eat. Other times I felt so guilty I just stooped in the shower and cried because I couldn't do anything right and all I wanted to do was at least just make one person happy with me. The borderline changed my truths so many times and the bipolar had me so high and low all the time that it's no wonder they couldn't get a diagnosis correct because I couldn't even figure out who I was. The older teenagers taught me everything I yearned to learn though, however inappropriate it was, and everything I needed to know about controlling my own pain the way I wanted to.

Considering this was an excruciating low point, I was overwhelmed at how disgusted I was with myself. I had just simply given up on everything…most of the time. As much as I wanted to let go, sometimes the borderline personality disorder in me would guilt me enough into hanging on. Sometimes my own lies made me believe that things were good. Other times, the borderline personality disorder would take the reigns and help to convince myself that everyone else was wrong, and that there really was nothing wrong with me. The best way I know to describe the feelings of going back and forth so drastically with personality is to say that it always feels like you are experiencing the best and worst of both worlds, and that you can't decipher from your own truths and your own lies sometimes. Sometimes I honestly tried to kill myself, and other times I would really try to find myself. By the time I felt like I was finding myself though my bipolar roller coaster would be too high or too low, and I'd realize that I was just a big nothing who deserved to die anyways! The combination of two illnesses unmedicated was nearly disastrous.

Day to day, hour to hour, I didn't know what direction I'd be going in. I would eat as many of the snacks and goodies as I possibly could after saving my vending machine stash for a week, and then purge it only moments later after feeling the guilt weighing me down as much as the calories. Again, I started starving myself until the doctors threatened me with the "weight shakes." These "shakes" were known among the anorexic and bulimic population of the hospital as the worst possible consequence, as apparently they added the most weight. I don't know if this theory of theirs was true or not, but I always gave in and ate before they had to give me the shake. I purged safely when they weren't checking me as closely. So, why did they care anyways? Once again. Back and forth. Mania. Depression. Mania. Depression. The only change was the environment. My insides and my life still felt the same as they had on the outside world, but I wasn't part of the outside world. I didn't belong anywhere. Why was it so much to ask? I just wanted to die!

I went into full self-destruct mode, and didn't care who noticed, except when the other side of the borderline in me wanted to impress people. I found myself so confusing, that it was just hard to live. At this point though, the major mood depressive disorder and the lows of bipolar disorder were the strongest driving points, so even my borderline personality disorder was all negatively focused. I found an earring and used it to pierce the skin that separates the thumb from the index finger. I angrily rug burned my knuckles until I could actually see what looked like tissue and bone fragment (where were the staff who were trained and paid to watch us during all this time?). Literally that must have taken near an hour, but I sat cross-legged on the floor and rubbed my knuckle back and forth for as long as I could physically move my wrist. I angrily rubbed because it made me hurt more physically than mentally, and that was the one thing that I felt like I could control. When I had finally self-medicated myself enough to not feel as angry, I stopped. Just like that. I stood up, walked away from the bloodstained carpet, and went to wash my hands. High. Low. Stop. Start. Good. Bad. Today I still have that scar on my ring finger knuckle, a visible reminder in many ways, of how far I've come. Years ago, I had acidic injections to attempt to reduce some of my scars without actual plastic surgery, but it never made a difference. Now though, I'm confident enough in myself that they don't bother me, but it did actually take a few years for me to get to that point. My life has just always seemed to be all one, or all of the other.

I hid from myself, told outrageous lies, adamantly refused to cooperate with anyone, and I just plain fell apart. In part, I now know that some of it was due to a bipolar crash but it was also obvious post traumatic stress disorder too, as I had been raped only six days prior to my admittance at Death's Doorway. The bipolar part comes in as I had already planned to kill myself for as long as I can remember so that wasn't necessarily connected to the rape, but the crash came in when I fantasized about how I would do it. How I would destroy my body completely because there were already too many parts that were damaged and needed to be destroyed, according to my logic. Remembering and revealing the rape AND my unmedicated mental illnesses was just too much to cope with. The major mood depressive disorder just guaranteed a ticket to the lowest depth of my roller coaster... AGAIN!

Daily we had to meet as a group for daily therapy sessions. Most of it felt irrelevant to me because I wasn't in high school, had never abused drugs, didn't have an anger management problem, and generally just refused to speak. They were aware of my cutting, rape experience, and molestation though, and tried to explore those areas with me a few times, but only to receive my silent response. They didn't ask questions, they just expected me to be able to discuss it as conversationally as I would the weather. I didn't know what to tell them because even I wasn't sure why cutting felt so good. I didn't want them to know that I was having flashbacks of the rape, and reliving it every time I so much as thought about it. I was afraid they would realize how deeply dark and disturbed I was if they knew that the only image my mind could conjure up anymore of the man who had molested me as a child was his penis. Not to mention, my other favorite outlets of grief; anorexia and bulimia. If they knew all of these things I decided that they would *really* know too much about me and *really* know how crazy I was. Any answer I could've come up with would've sounded crazy, but the action itself didn't feel crazy. The advice and lectures just seemed superficial coming from people who only wanted informational-pamphlet answers. I just hated life and didn't belong anywhere, I thought. Easiest avoidance method – silence!

The therapists always selected the topics for these sessions, and their general responses did not seem like they would be effective in my world. To me, their responses and scenarios were too textbook. For example, their response to a patient about his lack of anger management control was for him to just tell someone that he didn't like their actions instead of beating the hell out of them. Just say, "I don't like it," when you find a girlfriend cheating, when someone hits you, when other kids pick on you, or any other time where your natural response may be physically confrontational. Obviously that's the best and most logical choice, but that doesn't mean it's a natural or a teachable response if you have a specific mental illness. Another example was the counselors discussion more geared towards sexual abuse. They would remind us that it wasn't our faults, regardless of whether it was a family member or not. They would tell us that their perpetrators got what they deserved as according to the law, that we made the right choice to tell. They even suggested that one day we would feel more at ease with it and wouldn't hurt so much. I *didn't* feel like my perpetrators got what they deserved. I was living what my perpetrators deserved by realizing what a terrible, unfixable person I was. I may have made the right choice to tell, but it didn't make me feel any *better*. With anorexia and bulimia, they would just remind me of how much my body needed the food and the health risks of both; however, that was the last thing I cared about when my mind was focused on forcing outside pain on my body! Due to my experienced cutting and self-mutilation, I also had a wide array of scars. A few on my knuckles from the hour I spent grinding it into the carpet, one on another knuckle I had smashed into bone fragments during a wall punching episode, several slits and slice scars up, down, and across both of my arms, the word DIE on one ankle, a heart with a piercing arrow on the ankle, and several scars just as a result of scratching. They lectured me that one day I would regret the scars so I shouldn't self mutilate. They should've known better! I wished to die, so telling me how to live wasn't exactly *listening* to what I was silently screaming!

They always loved to try to get me to crack, but I was never able to talk. I just wanted to dissolve into the floor. Inside I may have been manic, eagerly planning and dreaming for my next scheme for how I was going to cut next. The euphoria of thinking about where I would do it, how good it would feel, what part of my body I would choose to use as my outlet where I cut. Still I would sit in these torturous therapies surrounded by people I didn't know, silent. "Tell us about it," they would encourage, but the words felt too crazy to say, so I just couldn't. Inside I may have been "at the bottom of the barrel" depressed, plotting my escape plan and how I would kill myself by jumping in front of an oncoming car since my plan was to break free at night. Again, I would remain silent. They would ask me to talk about the rape. "Tell us all what happened." Even as an adult, I think, "are you kidding me?!?!" I wouldn't sit around with my colleagues now and talk about being raped. How was it therapeutic to talk to strangers, several of who could not relate or didn't care, supposed to make me feel better? They wouldn't even ask me why I wanted to kill myself. They just said that I should tell someone if I was feeling that way. If it were only that easy.

I hated that! The lies! They may have been accredited or had degrees, but if those things had never happened to them, how could they understand exactly how to help me? Just because you've read the research doesn't mean that you've felt the feelings. People who are troubled or have been hurt need more *compassion*, *understanding*, and *listening*. What I needed was for them to tell me was that it was ok to still feel guilty, as it is a normal part of the grieving and growing process. I needed to hear that it was still okay to love the offender because of the positive feelings and memories also often times instilled by that person. They needed to also tell me in those discussions how to handle living outside the hospital, possibly having to deal with the consequences of making the "right choice" for getting help. They could have told me how to feel safe walking down the hallways of school despite the stares from classmates, and how to feel safe in life, with strategies to avoid future abuse or rape. What I needed from them was help and hope.

One thing that became clear to me though my therapy sessions at Death's Doorway was that all touching was bad. Obviously they knew the details of the rape and molestation, and my other promiscuous behaviors with the Jerk prior to the rape, so they worked hard at getting the message across to me that all touching from boys or men was bad and horrifically wrong. It was ingrained within my mind that anytime someone touches you, it is bad not to tell! With this in mind, my mind reeled at any and all of the interactions I had ever had with any males before in my life. Had I been abused on other occasions and didn't recognize it as abuse? Had someone else violated me, and I just didn't know because I hadn't known the rules about touching? I wish I could blame my next actions on my naïve questioning and unknowing about touching appropriately verses inappropriately, but that logic is only partially to blame. After that, the borderline in me just took over. Borderline isn't something you can necessarily tell when you are going back and forth because everything you say and think *really* feels real. It's not a matter of being honest or dishonest, it is a matter of believing your own dishonesty. I was convinced that my dad had sexually abused me.

With a little encouragement from *now* eager to *listen* staff, who seemed more like excited news reporters, I accused my dad of more than twenty charges of abuse. As a result unmedicated bipolar disorder, my borderline disorder tendencies flourished. I just *knew* those charges were true. Due to the newness of all of the information to the staff, they only encouraged me to keep talking. It was like adding fuel to a fire. The more they gawked, the more I came up with. As an unmedicated bipolar, the borderline in me came out significantly more often. Of course my dad had never committed any of those charges. My mom, my final admittance, and a full investigation proved that, but I honestly believed during the time I was retelling to the staff that it had actually happened. I had clear and precise details. I was a bipolar and borderline at her best! No matter what treatment, doctor, medication, or any other factor, they just couldn't stop the borderline personality disorder and bipolar disorder in me. They weren't targeting that though since they didn't have a diagnosis. They also didn't necessarily know that was what I was going through since I didn't have a diagnosis, but I just couldn't slow down and breathe. Mentally I was all over the place and I couldn't help it. I had gone from completely uncaring what the doctors and staff thought at all, to occasionally trying to please them. I just wanted it all to stop so I could be just one person without any roller coasters.

I both regarded and disregarded the rules and just cut when I wanted, but in the least noticeable areas. I attended the group therapy sessions, and then retreated to my room as often as I could (one of their "no no's"). I paid attention to the speeches from the doctors, and then knocked a hole in the wall at night so that I could suck the guy's dick who resided in the room next to mine. I took the medications, but said, "fuck you" to the teachers and staff if I just didn't want to do something. I would participate in therapy, but then punch a whole in the wall or throw something at the nurses when I got pissed off. I was experiencing all worlds, personalities, mood swings, and all were overwhelming, and overlapping all at once. I just had finally reached the point where I had given up and didn't care. I cried in my time-limited showers, at least attempting to hide how much my life was killing me. I just couldn't handle myself and was silently screaming to get out.

Remember the "best" child psychiatrist in town that I previously mentioned? Well, he finally came up with a solution to fix me. He decided that I needed to be locked in a ward completely by myself in order to learn to not be so manipulative and to learn to have more concern about my own treatment. The next day I was locked in a ward completely by myself. I only had a one-on-one aide who had to be within touchable contact (T.C.) of me at all times, as opposed to V.C. (visible contact). My lesson was to suffer with constant and permanent touch contact. Touch Contact (T.C.). and Visual Contact V.C. were supposed to be used to monitor a residents safety if there was any question of self harm, or if someone was a new and questionable patient, but they were often used as punishments too. I had been banished to an entire floor by myself with only a one-on-one aide for an entire month! In other words when I peed, she was always close enough to wipe for me! Not that I would've ever allowed that or not that she would've tried, but that's how close she always was to me. Doctor Bullshit decided that this was the best form of "Treatment" for me because all I needed was to learn not to manipulate. We were also restricted to only talking about my behaviors, choices, and experiences. She was ordered, and refused to talk to me about anything else, so most of our time was spent by my yelling at her and her refusal to speak to me. I wasn't even allowed to eat with any of my peers. My meals were brought to me to eat alone in my single occupant entire floor ward. I didn't go to the linens closet anymore to collect my towels. I didn't go to the washer and dryer machines to do my laundry anymore. I was completely removed from all interactions. This was my punishment; not a lesson! I lived this way until they gave up on me, and released me.

The lesson was meant to teach me to quit manipulating people, but again, they never asked. Sure I was smart enough to manipulate people, but the truth was simple. I wasn't manipulating, I was trying to deal with a raging roller coaster and varied personality quirks in my mind that were speeding out of control. I wasn't manipulating people, I was trying to decide how I could handle being the same person for each moment; angry, sad, hurt, happy, depressed. I didn't just feel emotions naturally. My emotions all centered around my inner roller coaster, personality for the moment, anxiety, and level of depression. I could've found a way to tell them if they would've asked and listened to my silent screaming, I just didn't know how to start. I needed help...wasn't that why I was there?!?!

February 14, 1994: patient released due to minimal progress

Memorable Moments

When I was a teenager my mom also took my brother and I to the Olympic Games in Atlanta in 1996. What a magical experience! I didn't even care what events we saw, I was just over the moon happy to be there at all. The pulse of the crowd was palpable as everyone had their own excitements and thrills. What an amazing time! It seemed like the world of our lives stopped and we were living in The World of the Olympics, and that nothing else even existed. No one cared about anything else that was going on anywhere else in the world because Atlanta was the center of attention, and I was in the middle of it. The people all had the same looks that resembled the way I felt; transported to another planet called Olympics, and it was great!

I remember reading the Olympic Creed on a banner displayed on the wall of the pool facility, and getting goose bumps because it's implications were so strong and meaningful. It indicated a respect for talents, that everyone had talents, and to always strive to use and better these talents. I also wanted to see gymnastics, but of course as one of the most popular sports, we didn't get that choice either. We did see soccer, equestrian, synchronized swimming, and other events, but like I said before, it was the thrill of being a part of history and such excitement that was the power of being there.

The thrill of being among shoppers searching for the perfect Olympic memorabilia or souvenir was exhilarating. Despite being somewhat claustrophobic, I was ecstatic about being in such a huge crowd that all had a feeling of gratitude for being a part of something so huge. It was just a phenomenal experience! Even though I was old enough to find my brother annoying, it was one of the family vacations that I remember us all being so happy and excited (not to mention busy) that we never even argued. We just loved being together and sharing something so special together. I have a picture of my mom, my brother, and I standing in the middle of Olympic Village and when I think about that trip, all I see is the warmth and happiness that was reflected in the picture.

Help Me

Make me feel normal
Bring peace to my life
Help me remember
How it feels not to cry.
I begged for a cure,
when they said "nothing's wrong,"
They said I'd improve,
But I'd felt this bad all along.
The rights medications will help
and we care for you too
But how much did they care
when their medications didn't do
the tricks they wanted them to?

Age 15

CHAPTER 10

Home Sweet Home

I was released on Valentines Day. Such irony considering the heart carving I made into my ankle just before being admitted! A heart carved on my ankle to mark my entrance, and the holiday of hearts with my broken spirit to mark my departure from Death's Doorway. The day of love, happiness, kindness, sweethearts, and loving thoughts, and I left dressed in black thinking about morbidity, death, carving into myself, taking the pills I had come to love so much, calling my old time guy friends as soon as I could to go get in trouble again...not at all in a Valentines Day mood. I was bipolar! I was happy to get out and try to stay safe, but I also couldn't wait to find the closest trouble possible. I was ready for it all now...sex and drugs too! I had learned enough in the hospital that I couldn't wait to try. Why the hell not? It wasn't like I was a virgin anyways! I never had the choice of losing my virginity, and my mind, heart, and soul were too fucked up to be fixed obviously, so why not? I didn't have anything to lose anyways.

I was thrilled to be getting out of Death's Doorway, but I was scared. It was still during the school year, and I wasn't allowed to return to school because of the day I took a knife to school incident. I had been expelled as a result of the knife/suicide attempt. The biggest reason I was happy to come home (although I sure wouldn't have admitted it at the time) was because I missed my mom so much while I locked up. There were actually times that I cried in my bouts of bipolar lows because I missed her nagging me about my room or getting mad at me because I stayed out too late. There was so much that I had missed about her; however, coming home also felt like stepping into an unfamiliar world. I had grown in negative ways as I had learned more about dangerous life altering mistakes, but I wasn't prepared for my mom, brother, or any of my other family members to have changed as well.

My family came religiously to visit me when I was at Death's Doorway, probably as often as they were allowed to, but while I was there time had stopped for me. Now all of the sudden I had to speed up six months, and I sure had a lot to catch up on. When I was at Death's Doorway, my family, especially my mom and grandma, would bring me McDonalds and pizza practically every time they came. They would bring things I was allowed to have like books, magazines, and other small things that I couldn't find a way to use to hurt myself with. The hospital was very strict about what was allowed at all. No shoelaces, jewelry, belts, bras with underwire…lots of "no," but my family always found a way to follow the rules and still try to make me as happy as they could, considering I was an angered, misdiagnosed, and miserable teenager.

I'll never forget the time my mom brought a kitten to the visit with her. She and my brother had adopted the kitten, and she was determined that I get to play with it while it was young, so she brought it to the hospital. I know it was important to her that I still be a part of the family, so she brought it the same week they picked him out. Believe it or not, the demonic workers at the hospital actually let me go outside with my mom for five minutes to play with the kitten. With the leash in hand, we walked (or more like dragged, since cats don't like leashes) the kitten outside so I could pet, play, and snuggle the newest member of the family. The new member who had replaced me. The new member who came to my home when I wasn't even living there. Stupid to think all that just because of a cat, I know, but I was misdiagnosed and unmedicated, so everything troubled me. I did love the kitten though, and as far as motivation goes, it worked. For the slightest of times, it was enough to encourage me to try to get a *little* better, even though I didn't really have the treatment help that I needed to do so.

As an adult I have to laugh at the image of my mom and I playing with a kitten on a leash in the front small grassy area of a nuthouse. I was rolling around with it trying to get it to chase pine needles and my mom was holding the leash trying to get it to play with or bite the leash. We walked him in circles momentarily and then giggled when he was a little dizzy, and we took turns holding him, as much as a kitten will in a strange environment. To onlookers, I wonder which one of us they thought was the resident since the idea itself made both of us look crazy!

Nonetheless I came home and honestly tried to make the best of it at first. All my friends obviously knew what happened, especially since the rape was in the newspaper and because I had been out of school for so long. My use to be best girl friend had been forbade to see me, since I was a bad influence. I still didn't have anything except a family who had grown six months without me. I was watched more closely. People thought differently about me. People treated me differently. People acted differently around me. No matter if I was manic or low, it drove me crazy. I just wanted to either be happy or die. It seemed like I couldn't do either right. I was watched so closely I couldn't kill myself, and I couldn't be happy because it hurt so much to be happy and disguised. I felt like I, and my emotions, were always on display and I didn't like it or know how to handle it.

Since I was expelled and my mom had to work, I rode my

bike to my grandparents every day. It was the safest option, since everyone knew that I needed careful watching. Being with my grandparents was a simple solution. I would be watched closely, and they weren't too busy to take the time to care for me. Despite my troubles, I know a part of me, grandma, and paw enjoyed some of the time we spent together when we were all actually able to forget how many problems I had. That was one of the best times I had with paw. No one knew what to do with me, so he just treated me normally. He spoiled me, as he always had, and didn't even let on that he knew anything was different. We went to arcades, he paid for private gymnastics lessons, took me to bookstores and toy stores, and took me for ice cream anytime I asked. For a punishment due to expulsion, he was exactly what I needed to realize that I wasn't such a bad or crazy person after all. To him, no matter what anyone said, I was just his precious first born grandchild.

Some inner demons I just couldn't let go of though. I continued to cut, binge and purge, and alternate with anorexia. I just still felt so miserable inside that I needed something, yet again, to control my inner pain. Forcing pain on the outside somehow seemed to relieve the inner pain, at least temporarily. It also gave me a chance to focus on things I could control. I couldn't control being lonely, without any friends. I couldn't control having been hospitalized for so long. I couldn't control feeling guilty, too high, too low, too different. It felt like there were a million things that I couldn't control. With the self destructive behaviors I held onto though, I felt like I still had some form of control. I also continued to try to reaffirm my old friendships with the people who I knew were not healthy for me – obviously not the rapist though! I wanted so badly to be fixed. What might have started before as a demonstration of attention getting behaviors based on real diagnostic problems, had now become an array of disguises I depended on in order to live freely. I couldn't even handle the freedom though because I was too locked up within my own mind,

No matter the normalcy my family tried to help create for me, the unmedicated bipolar took over, and I couldn't handle it yet again. The tendencies of the unmedicated borderline personality disorder controlled me still, and my stability still depended on who I was and what I was feeling. Even though I had all the family support one could possibly ask for, with mental illness, love just isn't enough. I knew they were trying, I was trying, but I just couldn't do it. I felt too out of place, and still didn't feel like I belonged anywhere. I just couldn't be successful at any capacity of a normal life. I dated a guy I had known from the hospital, and that ended badly, so I couldn't even date the way teenagers were supposed to without being reminded of how crazy I was (as he said when he dumped me). I needed to get back into the hospital where everyone could accept that you were hopeless and helpless. No matter how well or how poorly things were going in my life, I just couldn't handle the inner bipolar roller coaster. I did the only thing I could think of that would get me back in as soon as possible. Another suicide attempt.

In front of my entire family, I grabbed a steak knife and just started sawing at my wrists. As an adult it was one of the scariest and guiltiest moments of my life because of all the people I hurt in that single action. Too many people I truly love were my audience as I tried yet again to end my life as viciously and roughly as I could. My brother was nine and he had to watch his sister slash her wrists while my grandmother tried to rush him out the door in tears so that he wouldn't see anymore. My mom, stunned, started crying and begging me to stop. My granny and grandfather fought and wrestled to get the knife from me. Blood dripping, gushing, and spurting from me wrists, my mom called Death's Doorway again. The result, however, this time was surprising. Death's Doorway refused to accept me as a patient because I would not progress there, as proven in the past. I couldn't believe I was even a reject at a nuthouse now. How low can you go? Nobody wanted me.

Memorable Moments

My grandmother and granny on my mother's side of the family always had an annual trip to strawberry picking farms. My grandma, granny, mom, and I would squeeze into the car together for the long ride. Grandma always knew the best time in season, the best place to go, and the best way to go about it. Once we arrived at the strawberry farm, I loved seeing the horses and other animals, but couldn't wait to get my basket and start picking the freshest strawberries you had ever seen. I always knew the rules; no picking the green ones, no eating them because they hadn't been washed, and don't pick any that have gone bad. Most of the rules weren't a problem, but I couldn't resist eating a few because they were the juiciest, sweetest, and best strawberries we ever had every year. Considering we weren't supposed to eat them, I had to be sneaky about it. When no one was looking I stuffed the biggest strawberry I had picked into my mouth. The only way I could think to hide the evidence was to throw the green leafy top over my shoulder. It would've worked too if it hadn't landed on my granny's back! I remember so many endearing times going to my grandma, granny, and paw's house. They instilled a lifetime and sense of beauty to me in some of the most unlikely places. I often spent the night with them, and thought it was so exciting to push the twin beds together and sleep next to my grandmother. Other times, paw and I would empty his change drawer and play with the money. When I was small enough, we played hide and seek and I always hid in the sliding banistered part on his bed frame. Grandma always had the best collection of buttons too. My favorites were the ones that were the animal and fruit shaped ones. She kept them in a huge can with pictures of the circus around it. It was almost like a treasure. Grandma would read my favorite books as many times I wanted to hear them, and paw would set up the tent in the backyard so we could pretend to camp at dinner time.

My granny was one of the most unique women I have ever

known. She peeled apples all the way without the peeling even breaking once. She knew and could do everything! My grandma always knew how to handle my roller coaster, regardless of how long it took to get a diagnosis; what a strong woman! Paw was the goldmine of the family; *all* kids loved paw!

Who Cares What Happens?

Just one time
won't hurt me at all.
Just one hit of acid.
Who cares if I fall?
Just one more time.
I need it right now.
Who cares if I'm addicted?
It just calms me down.
Just one little sniff
of the powdered cocaine.
No harm done at all.
No one cares – it feels just the same.
Just one little pinch.
The needle can't hurt.
One minute I feel fine.
The next I know I'm only worth dirt.
Just end it all.
No one cares anyways.
Just pick a day and date,
and pick your own way.

Age 17

CHAPTER 11

Heaven's Or Hell's Gate?

*S*ince Death's Doorway refused to help me, my mom had to find another way to get inpatient help for me. I was swearing to kill myself, so it wasn't like she could just take me home. She must have been exhausted with her love for me, but at the same time, it must have been easier on her to know that someone could protect me twenty-four hours a day and seven days a week. Not to mention she was an outlet for all of my pain, and one personality actually enjoyed causing her so much grief. Of course what I didn't know at the time, and didn't have the capacity to understand was that she was going through hell with the insurance companies. Since I didn't have an official diagnosis, it was hard to justify to them why I needed such extensive and expensive therapy. She fought for me in so many ways, I was just too disturbed and incorrectly diagnosed and medicated that I didn't know or care.

The next alternative to Death's Doorway was a residential

treatment center an hour and a half from our home. It had the same *real* name as Death's Doorway because they were a related chain of hospitals but to this day, I still cannot decide if the second hospitalization did more good or more harm for me; hence the chapter title. Did they *really* help me? No. Did they *really* hurt me? No. The difference was that at Death's Doorway in my town, people just looked away when they knew something was wrong. Here, at Heaven's or Hell's Gates, people pushed and pushed because they thought it was the right thing to do. Maybe it was, and maybe it wasn't, but it least it sent the message the someone cared. They challenged us to do everything, and didn't give us much of a choice. The consequences were more appropriately and consistently applied. In my experience there, the time out room was so bad that I never gave them an opportunity to have to use any of the other consequences.

Right from the beginning, I figured I was a professional resident at treatment centers now, so why not walk in and act like you own the place? Wrong! They were very strict, restrictive, and mean in some cases when it really was deserved. Not condoning that treatment as far as the meanness is concerned, but sometimes everyone needs a taste of their own medicine. It was my choice to be there, after all. I had knowingly slashed my wrists and tried to kill myself right in front of my own family. I knew being institutionalized was inevitable as a result, and of course had the roller coaster of bipolar emotions that came along with it. It was my maddening bipolar that once again led me to the lows of needing institutionalization, but again, they wouldn't get a correct diagnosis yet. I don't know that I ever heard them mention any other diagnosis other than the possibility of schizophrenia. They always seemed to talk around me, and not too much to me. I didn't know my goals, where as the other hospital wrote daily goals for us. Of course we didn't care about them, but here, I had no idea what to do or expect.

On my first day I was already sent to the time out room. Who the hell cares I thought, because again, I was an expert at the padded rooms too. Once I got to their timeout room though, I was immediately surprised. Gone was the padding. Gone was the solid door with a slit for a window. This room was solid gray, all hard concrete stones, and had a gate that looked more like a prison cell than a time out room. It didn't take me long for me to learn that I was going to control my behavior enough to try to avoid that room. Already I had developed a phobia of small places, as a result of my over frequent visits to the time out room at Death's Doorway, but this new time out room would have given me have a nervous breakdown compared to the other one I had been in. I was only in the concrete dungeon once. I made sure of that! I knew enough to know already that I really didn't like it here though. This wasn't going to be near as easy as Death's Doorway was. I figured that out early on and it only made my bipolar and borderline struggle even more. I didn't like it there at Heaven's or Hell's Gate, but I couldn't handle being at home. I just didn't like anyone, anything, or anywhere. What next?

The entire place was different. We actually had to wake up at a certain time, make our beds a certain way, have hall and bathroom monitors, and line up accordingly for breakfast. It wasn't a choice, it was our drill sergeant routine. We never had such a stringent routine at Death's Doorway, which leads me to the question was this place Heaven for me due to the possibility of help, or was it just a deeper level of hell? Again, I know that they at least made decisions based on what they thought would be best for us instead of just not caring. I wasn't working with my normal psychiatrist or therapist either, so it was all very new. Heaven's or Hell's Gate was certainly led and run more similar to a juvenile detention center as opposed to my stay at Death's Doorway. Obviously the bipolar again changed my opinions and emotions regularly as I continued to live on a roller coaster.

My cocktail of medications was changed though, and visitation was not allowed as often as it was at Death's Doorway. Again, more things that led me in the right direction, or things that hurt me even worse? At "Heavens or Hell's Gate", we were not given things. Everything we received we had to earn based on points and demerits. We had to attend every therapy session and were either given demerits or points based on our interactions and participation. We also had regularly scheduled chores that worked on a rotation level and a hall monitor that was one of the residents who was in charge of previewing before the staff approved our rooms, dress, and chore completion. Again, either demerits or points.

Some days I cared and really did a great job following the rules because it felt good to do something right, and I loved the praise. Other days I would hate everyone, and do everything wrong on purpose. I'd push the limits as far as I could, but not too far – I was determined not to go back to that gray dungeon time out room. I didn't "feel" back and forth on purpose. I just couldn't help it. Nonetheless, I couldn't control the unmedicated bipolar in me there, and they didn't pick up on it either.

I was not at this hospital long enough to remember exactly how the points and demerits system worked, but I did learn really quickly that you did not want demerits. This place made me *really* want to go home. At the facility at my home town, my first hospital, we were allowed to make our choices (watch t.v., sulk in our rooms, listen to music, do puzzles, read, board games, etc.). At this place we had to earn those things. We had to earn anything and everything, all the way down to desserts at dinner. At my first facility we had a checklist that indicated the behaviors we did or didn't have throughout the day. At this facility though, my second one, we had a chart that kept number of our points or demerits. We were constantly being rewarded for earning enough points, or missing out on privileges for receiving demerits. I don't know how it was possible, but they even managed a daily outside time for those who earned enough points. It was in a wire fenced in yard, similar to a prison, and it was only for fifteen minutes, but we always worked for things like that because it was all we had. I hated it but somehow I was mature enough to realize their well intentioned attempts, although it still did not get me a correct diagnosis or on the right track. I wasn't even at this hospital long enough to remember my therapist's or doctor's names.

When I mentioned earlier that we were required to attend and participate at all therapies, I really did mean *all* of them! We had physical, occupational, drug and alcohol, abuse/rape, anger management, and coping therapies. Somehow they managed to squeeze these in daily, but again, it was the points and demerits that kept everyone going. If someone wanted to be able to watch a 30 minute t.v. program he practically had to behave perfectly at everything, so most of us at least attempted. Most of the therapies only offered information I had either read about in a brochure, heard from my therapist or Doctor Bullshit, or heard in a session at Death's Doorway, so it wasn't overwhelmingly memorable.

There was, however, one part of physical therapy that I will never forget though because it was one of the moments that my mania and lows seemed to strongly overlap. I was use to one or the other of my many levels of moods, but I wasn't used to them overlapping so intensely. The stimulation of the Ropes Course physical therapy at Heaven's or Hell's Gates put me all over the bipolar mood map though, as far as my emotional roller coaster was concerned. I'm sure it was also to teach us to trust, try, believe, and other positive character traits, but I never felt much of that. It is only as an adult in reflection that I realize they had intended it to be more than just a physical workout. For Ropes Course we had to do various things. Most of them were very challenging, very demanding, and even somewhat scary. For one, we literally had to try to walk along two tight ropes tied between the two tallest trees. We climbed up nail pegs in the trees to reach the top, and had to slide our feet along the tightropes as far as we could. We had safety harnesses and a inpatient peer holding the other end of the harness on the ground, but tell me, how safe would you feel one hundred feet in the air with another crazy person holding the rope that is attached to your life? I may have wanted to kill myself, but this damn wasn't how I wanted to do it. This whole experience scared me to death!

Another ropes course activity was to climb to the top of a pole (power line pole of course not attached to wires) again using the nail pegs to climb. We wore the same harness and were challenged to climb to the very top. Once we were on top, we were just supposed to jump wildly and freefall, while our peer on the ground slowly lowered the harness until we were safely at the ground. Again, how safe would you feel? My bipolar roller coaster was all over the place. I was manic with the risk taking, and 100% depressed because I was scared, and hated letting any fear seep out and become obvious to anyone. I remember reaching the top, and deciding that there was no way in hell I was going to jump. I even remember yelling down to the therapists, staff, and other inpatients below that they might as well order pizza or something because it was going to be a long time before anyone in their right mind could convince me to jump. As far as I was concerned there wasn't anyone there who was in their right mind so, plain and simple, I wasn't coming down. I don't know how long I spent at the top of that pole, carefully seated at the top. I don't remember how in the world they convinced me to jump. Maybe I just finally got tired of sitting and waiting, and became bored. Once you climbed up, it was nearly impossible to climb down, trust me, I certainly tried. Finally, I jumped. What surprised me was that it as the best bipolar manic feeling in the world. It was the perfect feeling. The freefall freedom, just before dying if you choose to leave the world by jumping from anything. It gave me new and refreshed zeal to "get better", get the hell out of this place, and "just chill it out" for a while. Finally then I would be able to follow through with the perfect suicide since both my real and attention getting suicide attempts kept being destroyed.

I will never forget when my female therapist called me into her office for another one of our sessions. I wasn't even at this hospital to even remember what she specifically looked like. I didn't have anything important to say, so I just followed along numbly ready to waste the hour. As soon as we got in, we started with the usual questions. How have you been feeling? Have you had any self-injurious thoughts? Have you had any suicidal thoughts? On and on these questions continued until she paused, I imagined, just to take a break from my nonchalance. I knew they never listened. This place was no different in that regard. We were just teenagers. What did we think or know about life or the world? At least they pretended to care by asking realistic questions.

"We have been communicating with your mom about the need for you to be in a state hospital. We think that you have an illness that we cannot help you with, so we are looking into availability of state hospitals. You would be there until you were eighteen, but no longer covered by insurance after that. Your behaviors indicate that you are psychotic and need a more permanent placement." You would think you would remember the exact image of someone who said something so unbelievable, but all I remember feeling was fear. "Oh shit," I thought. I didn't care if I really was crazy enough to need it. There was no way I was going to be locked up for the next four years. The lesson that I learned was to disguise my feelings better, show them what they wanted to see, and hope it wasn't too late to convince them that I could go home. I didn't know if time was on my side or not. The therapist said that they were only waiting for a slot to open in a state hospital in Texas.

This news sent me off the bipolar charts. I was so manic that I was a perfect resident. OR I was so low that I secretly scratched in areas they wouldn't notice, ate meals only to purge in the bathroom later, and wrote poems about death, but I made sure they didn't see that side of me anymore. I hated myself. I hated that I couldn't understand or stop the roller coaster. Shouldn't it have been easier, I wondered? All I wanted was to get out of this place and stay as far as possible from a state institution, but I couldn't even manage to pull off the false "I'm cured" without my roller coaster getting in the way. Sometimes when I cut deep enough, I would imagine that I was ridding myself of the darkness inside me so that I wouldn't have to deal with such drastic emotions all of the time. I gave up complete hope of finding a normal or real way to ever feel healthy, and focused completely all around on becoming a lifelong fake in disguise.

Memorable Moments

One of the many times I went to visit my aunt and uncle, specifically when my cousin and I were at the age where we loved out precious baby dolls, brings to mind an incident that still brings a smile to my face to this day. My cousin and I each took our dolls everywhere with us; to the breakfast table, outside, to the restroom, even on walks. One evening in the dusk light, my cousin and I, along with our baby dolls, were catching tadpoles outside in the ditch next to their yard. Suddenly we heard ducks and were over the moon excited! We grabbed our babies and ran into the house. We weren't allowed to walk away from the house without an adult, so we just had to bring my aunt along so that we could see the ducks. Even at eight months pregnant, even she was a little excited at the prospect of seeing ducks and ducklings.

My cousin and I walked about twenty feet and the sound got louder. We were close, and we knew it. As my aunt neared us, we waited for her so that we could all peek in there to see the family of ducks. My cousin and I gently parted the branches and saw a family. It wasn't quite the family we expected though. We saw the most, and the biggest toads I have ever seen in my life. Squealing with surprise, my cousin and I took off running towards my aunt and uncle's house, completely forgetting that she was pregnantly chasing and supervising us. We laugh about it now, but my aunt's biggest phobia in the world is frogs and toads, so imagine the predicament we left her in.

My aunt is the glue that helps to hold me together during my lowest of lows. For an incredible amount of time, she has been my rock and one of my biggest supporters. How lucky and fortunate am I to have such a special and amazing family? To this day my aunt is one of my biggest supporters, and definitely helps to hold me together when I am struggling. She is an amazing woman, and has helped me become the person I wanted to become.

It Can't Happen To Me

Injecting a needle,
and withholding a cry.
The young girl awaits
for her everyday high.
She's running from fear
of another institution.
Considering the need for money,
Hmmmm…Street prostitution?
She'll always be paying
for the choices within
to a world full of drugs
where the pain never ends.
And for whatever reasons
this girl wants to die.
She's forgetting it all
and ending her life.

Age 18

CHAPTER 12

Can I Make It This Time?

*S*ince I knew that my next hospital would be a permanent placement, I was determined to hide and disguise how I felt as much as possible. I didn't care how much my insides were screaming for help, I certainly sure wasn't going to show it and end up in a state hospital. The very thought of living in a hospital for the next four years was unbearable since I knew from experience that hospitals couldn't really help me. I had been in extensive therapy for a very long time, and personally didn't feel any progress. I had been prescribed so many medications that I had probably been on all of them, at one point or another. Literally, every technique, medication, and therapeutic strategy had been tried on me, but I gave up, let go, and concluded that I was just plainly unfixable.

I would have to live with the roller coaster, not knowing when or where it would strike me, or how high or low it would take me. I had to live not knowing if I would be my typical self, or if I would unknowing slip back into the someone else who occupied my body

143

from time to time. I had to live with the constant anxieties about everything; my clothes, my impressions on others (good or bad), my emotions, my life…simply everything. Either I had to live with these things, or I had to die. I chose death, but I knew I would have to trick people for a while before I got a real chance. I played their game of "recovery" and secretly plotted my plans to rid myself of this cruel world once and for all. There was going to be no turning back finally, because I didn't want to live in a state hospital, at home, or anywhere else so being dead was the only place I wanted to be. Only sometimes though. It just depended on the roller coaster.

As much as I did not want to go to a state hospital and as hard as I tried to get released from Heaven's or Hell's Gate, I actually do not remember the specific events that led up to my being released. I do not even remember the specific date. I'm sure there is some symbolism somewhere in why I remembered my release from the first hospital so vividly and do not have any memories at all of preparing to leave or actually leaving hospital number two. The only reason I can think of in reference to why my memories have faded from leaving Heaven's or Hell's Gates is because it didn't necessarily matter. I desperately wanted to avoid a state hospital so it didn't matter what day it was to me. I just wanted out, and hoped to ensure that they would never be able to capture me by recognizing my insanity ever again.

It was the end of the summer of the year when I was expelled and nearing my ninth grade year. My "normal" peers were going shopping to get ready for high school, learning to wear make up, beginning to date, talking for hours at a time on the phone, and so many other things I wasn't doing. I didn't have any friends. Anyone I would've chosen as a friend would not have been someone my mom would've let me be friends with since I was being so closely guarded. I never got an eighth grade yearbook. I was expelled, so I did not get to attend the eighth grade prom. Even though I completed the courses through the hospitalizations and had a homebound tutor, I was expelled, so I didn't even get to attend my eighth grade graduation or prom. I missed the finale of my middle school experience so I really had no idea what to expect in high school and I didn't have anyone to ask. On my manic or good days I was excited and scared, but eager to start a new chapter in my life (notice I didn't say new beginning yet!). When I was at the lowest of my lows, again thanks to being bipolar, it made me nervous, terrified, and anxious, which only gave me even more urgency to kill myself before the horrifying experience started.

The summer was uneventful, but I was closely monitored and medicated (although psychiatrists still hadn't come up with a correct diagnosis or medication). I could barely pee without someone getting worried, let alone find anything to kill myself with. Believe me I searched hard, but found nothing. No knives at all, no razors for shaving legs, no string even to try to form into a rope. To add insult to injury, even the pills were hidden and locked up. Damn, everyone was just so determined to keep me from doing the only thing I wanted to do. Even when I was manic, it was always in my mind still because I knew what would follow the mania. Another gut wrenching low. Over and over the cycle repeated, and just never stopped.

On the first day of ninth grade, my new chapter of life at high school, my pet hamster died. I should've considered that a predecessor as to what to expect because the rest of the year didn't get too much better. I had been away for so long and forgot how much my peers knew of my personal life. I had already picked up my class schedule and knew where to find most of my classes. I knew the general whereabouts around the school, but was terrified of high school because I knew I was stepping back into yet another world that didn't understand me. The world of my peers was always the cruelest to outsiders. I was avoided like the plague. "There's the crazy girl who tried to off herself," I would hear girls snicker as they changed books from their lockers in between classes. No one sat with me at lunch, so I just didn't ever bother eating. I hid, which was all I ever wanted to do anyways.

Teachers were scared and angry towards me, having read my file and having been filled in on my past middle school experience. That didn't help any, so I just tried to disappear as much as possible. I sat in the back of all my classes, went strait from one class to another in order to avoid the hurtful things people said about me in between classes, and I made all A's the entire year just to be able to mentally say, "Fuck you all! I can be crazy, miss a whole year of school, make my death plans, and still prove that I'm smarter than you idiots!" I still left ninth grade with nothing though. No friends, make up, dates, …nothing but strait A's and the strong, seemingly constant urge to die.

As the year progressed and the students learned that I wasn't going to give them the pleasure of any exciting gossip and the teachers realized that I wasn't going to kill myself right there in the middle of their class, everyone eased up a bit. That was the most comfortable I was during the entire ninth grade year; when I was finally invisible! I began to enjoy things more, but I still had my roller coaster. I enjoyed swimming more, and was getting even better. I was winning more competitions than I ever had before. I had an art piece picked for the art show. I never ended up with a particular friend, but the year didn't end as miserably as it started. I still had my distinct personalities and highs and lows of bipolar, but it was a surprising calm after such stormy few years that I had prior to ninth grade.

I actually started to blossom because the people outside weren't feeling so aware of my every breath. I began to realize that my musical and swimming talents also carried over to my artistic side. As it turns out, I was a terrific artist, and formed a reliable bond with the art teacher who taught me for four years. During my lowest of lows he accepted my morbid art with sorrowful eyes, but praised me for my creativity. I know it sounds like he was just trying to overlook the problem, but at the time, his response was exactly what I needed. On the other hand, when I created something wonderful, he again praised my creativity. In other words he recognized my talent, challenged me to do my best, praised my effort instead of topic, and guided me to be the best artist I could. Art was a very strong, expressive, and healthy link for me in high school; second only to swimming.

I do not remember anything specific about the summer after ninth grade except that I took drivers ed. Big deal. Something changed though because when I started tenth grade, people started noticing me. And it wasn't for all my bad baggage either. Somehow over the summer, I had gone from the ugly duckling to the beautiful swan, and that opened the eyes of several people, however superficial the attention may have been. I had always been a swimmer, and started the high school swim team (as one of the best swimmers, I might add) in ninth grade. Now in tenth grade, swim team had a new meaning. People liked seeing me in a bathing suit. I joked along with my teammates at competitions and in the locker rooms in between practices. I made friends believe it or not! I was even keeping up my grades, so obviously my parents were happy with that too. Things were starting to look better, right? There was also a very elite group of girls at school that was a school designated club. Each year they received hundreds of applicants, but only few were selected to join. Ninth graders couldn't join. Two tenth graders, approximately ten juniors and seniors were invited to join each year too. Despite the fact that I was one of the only two tenth graders invited into *"the club"* (an obvious popularity contest), I still couldn't keep my roller coaster emotions in check, when I should've been at the top of the world. Outside things were great, but the inner turmoil of my mind always continued, so it didn't even lessen as the outside appearance of my life improved.

I was also accepted into the art club in tenth grade, which was another excitement for me, but still I just couldn't stay off that roller coaster of emotions. We got to help create and paint signs that were displayed all over the town for a variety of reasons. We got to design and paint signs to decorate the floats that were in the various holiday parades in our town. However mundane these projects may have been, it gave me a project to focus on. Sometimes it felt like my insides were clawing their way to get my real emotions out, but the project gave me a direction. Add paint to brush. Stroke brush on board. Dip brush in paint. Repeat. Sometimes I just needed things like that to bring the storm of my emotions to a calm.

By now I had been in therapy for three years, and I was making progress considering I was still alive. As I aged and matured, I was more willing to realistically discuss my issues, so the therapy did prove to help. It helped me rid myself of the horrid flashbacks of the rape and molestation. It helped me develop strategies to attempt to avoid feeling suicidal, and definitely what to do if I was tempted to attempt it. I really had started moving beyond some of my most difficult experiences in my life, so I truly believed I was changing. My grades were good. I had friends. My parents were happy with me. My family was comfortable with me. Things didn't feel right, but they felt better than they had in a long time. As good as it was ever going to get anyways, I assumed. I thought that was enough, but years later, I found out that I still needed help.

Dr. Bullshit, on the other hand, was making no progress with me because he still refused to listen! I know I was a stubborn teenager, but I also should've had some input on myself, and he just couldn't handle that, I guess. He had me on anti-psychotics, anti-depressants, obsessive-compulsive medications, and ADD/ADHD medication since he charted that I documented behaviors indicating a need for even those type of medications. I had been on practically every type of medication in every family of medications involving mental health, but nothing seemed like the perfect fit or the perfect mix. It appeared as if I was doing better, but I was still not healthily sane I must admit. That much my mom did help me convince him of, even though he was still way off. He just wouldn't listen to me or my mom. As I have repeatedly mentioned, mental health hadn't evolved as much as it has up to this point, so possibly even the medications I needed may not have been as readily available. Even though bipolar disorder was a recognized illness, it still hadn't been a diagnosis that stuck with me. The only diagnosis that stuck was post traumatic stress disorder from the rape (which was greatly decreasing), depression, and manipulative teenager. I was smart enough to manipulate paint off a wall, but I wasn't trying to manipulate. I just couldn't control my feelings or emotions, so I couldn't always control the predicament it led me to. Nonetheless, I was in mostly honors classes in tenth grade, and proved to be a successful student and popularity contestant.

Memorable Moments

I remember when I was a child, one day a year the elementary school and work places coordinated and allowed a mother/daughter workday. Daughters were automatically excused from the day of school if they were going to go to work with their moms. I only got to do this once or twice since my mom had a job, which required a certain amount of confidentiality, but I will still never forget it.

All day I sat at my mom's desk drawing and coloring pictures, being the center of attention with the other ladies in her office, feeling like a "grown up" sitting and swirling in her big chair at her desk, and taking trips back and forth to the vending machine. I thought it was the coolest thing in the world that my mom worked somewhere that had a vending machine! Whenever my mom had to step out for confidentiality reasons, I felt so proud of her. Even though it regarded information that I wouldn't have understood anyways, it made me feel important to have a mom who was so important too. Someone trusted my mom with big secrets! Wow! They must know, just like I do, how great my mom really is. I loved the blinds in her office, and the narrow slits of sunlight that poured through. It was just a perfect day!

I know I am different

I wish I knew why I was different inside.
Sometimes I wish I could just leave and hide.
I know Im not like all the other kids.
When I do things they do I never feel like they did.
Sometimes I wish I could tell someone and be a baby and cry.
Because when I think about things I only think I want to die.

Age 7

CHAPTER 13

Let The Fun And Games Begin

High school so far had been relatively uneventful, but successful as far as my grades were concerned. My therapy sessions with my regular therapist lessened as time passed, but my medications were constantly changed as they didn't ever appear to be working. I had been seeing both my normal psychiatrist and therapist all along, with the exception of my out of town facility. I was doing well with my family and friends, and was happy that my dad had been able to move closer to our home town. He was still hours away, but not nearly as far as he had been. Either way, it meant that I could see him more often so I obviously looked forward to that. My highschool experience was completely divided into borderline personalities though, not to mention the highs and lows of bipolar. Half of it was a good student, who cared about friends, grades, and morals. This student loved pep rallies, attended on a regular basis, and valued the importance of my extracurricular activities. The other student was careless, reckless, and troublesome; the bad girl. Dark and serious, this student changed from the positive to the negative as drastically as the wardrobe of two completely different people would alter. This person wanted recognition for all the wrong things.

Sixteen was a hard age though because no matter who tried, my mom or my dad, I was just terrified of driving. Even after driver's ed, no amount of help or comfort seemed to help me. This was just one more thing that I could be angry with them about. One more reason why I could hate them. Everything was always someone else's fault when I was low. Between the typical teenage hormones, bipolar disorder, tendencies of borderline personality disorder, generalized anxiety disorder, and major mood depressive disorder, I was determined to let go and give up again. The driving experiences were just the surface problems. Behind closed doors though I would never admit how much driving scared me because I couldn't wait to get the freedom that came with driving. It wasn't that getting a car that made me change or want to change. I still didn't, and couldn't change. It was just that the freedom to be able to hide again was restored by my having a car. It also gave me easier access to trouble, but that would've never been a problem anyways since my friends all had cars too.

My mom did right when it came to car rules and night out rules, but during my eleventh grade year I finally pushed her so much that I don't know that I even gave her room to push back. My grades were still good enough, but I was finally introduced to drugs, as I had longed to be since I had first learned about them in the hospitals. I should've been scared of them because of all the stories I heard in the hospital, but that only made me want to try even more. For this reason, the first chance I had to try pot was in high school, and I eagerly did. Closely followed by LSD, Ecstasy, cocaine, hash, mushrooms, crystal meth, and crack.

I just couldn't get enough. It wasn't the drugs I was hooked to at first. It was the being myself and letting go that I was hooked to initially. I had tried so hard for years to be what everyone wanted. I really wanted to be that person too, but it seemed like no matter what I did, I just couldn't stay happy. Drugs gave me something exciting and new to think about, so I didn't have to think about being a screw up who couldn't really do it after all. After a few "better years" I just couldn't keep it together. Drugs made it easier to accept that too. I was a fuck up, so why not smoke, snort, and drink whenever I could. I looked good enough, was popular enough, and had enough friends so it was never costly for me. When I realized I could never be normal, drugs made me feel as normal as possible. Since no one understood how self-mutilating was my self-medication, I didn't expect anyone to understand how drugs did the same thing for me too. It did though, so I had no reason to try to stop it. All I had to be concerned with was hiding it, and it isn't very hard to hide anything if you are determined enough.

At sixteen, beginning eleventh grade, I acquired my first fake i.d. It said I was nineteen years old. Not old enough to buy my own booze, but at least old enough to get my own cigarettes, sign consent to get my belly button, tongue, and even my clit pierced, and get my first tattoo. Just as I loved the control I felt I had over myself by succumbing to drugs, having the fake i.d. made me feel like I had control enough of my life to make adult decisions, even though I wasn't an adult. Fact was, I was beginning a decade of the worst downward spiral I would ever have. It felt like the beginning of the end, and it almost was. The piercing and tattoo were the least of my problems, but they don't call certain drugs "gateway drugs" for no reason. The combination of drugs and unmedicated mental illnesses was nearly lethal for me. Drugs helped me escape reality, and made all the bad shit in my life go away, and the only things that mattered were completely imaginary. What a wonderful world to live in!

As for the drugs, yes, it was self-medication; however, at some point it was because I was completely hooked. It did start with marijuana, when I was sixteen. My best friend and I had rented a hotel room with my boyfriend at the time, and smoked a few joints. I giggled as I laughingly asked if I was stoned yet? It was the funniest feeling I had ever felt. No wonder people loved drugs so much, I thought. From then on, she and I smoked regularly and remained friends for years. For a while, that's all it took to add a little extra fun to bring me out of a low, or just to use when my borderline personality was to be the "bad girl". I loved the calmness that came with smoking pot. It helped me let go of the anxiety that was constantly eating away at my soul. It levitated me enough so that I didn't want to kill myself every second of every single day because I had too much stupid stuff to laugh about when I was stoned. It helped me feel that life wasn't so bad. It also negatively encouraged one or the other of the borderline personalities; because, one feeling was against it for the simple good Samaritan law-abiding citizen reasons, and the other feeling was the "bad girl" craving who didn't care. Smoking pot made me not care about which personality was dominating though, even if I had felt guilty about doing it all the way up to the moment I smoked it. Then I could be at peace and nothing else but my calmness mattered. My mind didn't race. I didn't feel guilty. I didn't feel manic or depressed. I just felt alive. At the same time, regardless of whether it's a physical or mental addiction, I continued to smoke pot until I absolutely had to quit, nearly a decade later.

LSD (acid) was a favorite of mine because it let you escape reality completely. I didn't have to care. I didn't have to think. Hell, half the time I didn't even know who I was, let alone did I care about anything. All I knew is that colors were brighter, the little blue Smurfs could talk to me, and everything was funny and unreal. It was the easiest carefree I've ever felt. The freeness of it was unrealistic. The freeness of it was what made me keep coming back to it again and again. Just like pot, it was a self-medication that harmed me for many years. LSD made me happy because it made my typical life feel unreal. It made my typical life of roller coasters, conflicting personalities, anxieties, and depression disappear. Just like that, nothing would matter and nothing would create or allow inner turmoil. For hours I could feel like anything. I could float on air. I could talk to animals. LSD made it so that the only thing that entered my mind was all the positives I felt I never had, or things I couldn't really do. LSD allowed me to forget that I knew there was something wrong with me. It allowed me to believe that my fantasy drug induced world was completely filled with happiness. There were no negatives with LSD and me, only positives. I have heard of people who have had "bad trips," but I cannot speak of that because I never did. I do not know if LSD is one of the mentally addictive drugs or not, but I do know that I became addicted to the disappearance of all negativity that constantly plagued my life.

I loved Ecstasy, but never had the chance to do it as often as I would've liked. It sent my bipolar disorder into direct and immediate mania. Since bipolar is so often influenced by sensory feelings and emotions, the physical feelings I had from Ecstasy made me want to continue feeling that way for the rest of my life. Every brush stroke through my hair felt magical. Every time I trickled my fingers down my arms, it would give me goosebumps and provide such a mental and physical relief and positive feeling. Wearing a soft robe, feeling the wind through your hair, making "snow angels" on clean sheets, feeling the waves crash between your toes, everything released such glorified feelings of inner peace and sensory passion that I really did love Ecstasy. The same applied with hash and mushrooms, as far as not getting to do them quite as much as I would've liked to at that particular time in my life. Like LSD, Ecstasy allowed me to enter a sensory Heaven, it seemed. My bipolar disorder has always neared mania the more my senses were heightened, so my happiness seemed to increase with these drugs. Ecstasy allowed me the freedom of happiness, both emotional and physically. Mushrooms also gave me feelings that were a combination of Ecstasy and LSD.

I snorted crystal meth and cocaine on several occasions, but only because it was there. I never felt any addictive powers of these drugs, I think, because my life already seemed to race. Considering these drugs are abused because people like the adrenaline, speeding, and racing, I wasn't so turned on by it. That didn't mean that I wouldn't do it though. I didn't get much from either drug, but anything that would kill me faster could only be a positive step, so I snorted it anytime I could. I can easily admit that I didn't have any addictive feelings to snorting either of these two drugs though.

Finally, at seventeen and I was making my own crack cocaine in a spoon over a lighter with "friends" well beyond my age. The smell of it, the immediate rush and brain gush you experienced from it, the intense pleasure, the sensation of your head and body floating…those few seconds after the sweet inhale of crack was beautiful. It was like the tinkling sound of wind chimes on a beautiful, cloudless, spring day all the while, having the best mental and physical feelings in the world. Crack was, by far, my favorite drug of choice. I came dangerously close to the edge of falling off when it comes to drug addiction. For days, weeks, months, I would hang out with a particular crowd who I knew would always have it around. I learned how to make my own, who to buy it from, how to cut it and sell it so that you could buy more for yourself. I learned it all, and I loved it all.

Crack was my vice. It felt so good. It allowed the brain relief from all thoughts, lightened the senses of the brain, but heightened the physical senses. It was the absolute best feeling I had ever experienced at time, and I simply couldn't get enough. It felt so good. It felt so powerful. Everything just felt great with the short crack induced happiness and numbness. I will never forget the power it had over my life, and how close I came to completely falling off and letting go because of its power.

My eleventh and twelfth grade years blur together. Not because I was on so many drugs, but because I was pretty enough to skip classes without getting in trouble or without my grades suffering, was popular enough that I didn't have any social concerns with teachers or students, was trained enough that my swimming didn't suffer, and at least came in and out of the house enough to reassure my mom that I was alive. The two years blend together because I did the same things for both years; sex, drugs, skipping school, partying, drugs, and being friends with the definite wrong crowd, so how could I distinguish between the two years other than my class schedules (which I didn't attend half of the time anyways).

My twelfth grade year was only more specifically defined by the positives of being a senior. I was selected to be among the few girls for our Miss High School Pageant. I was the captain of my swim team, and by far, the best female swimmer of the year. I was the "big fish in a small pond" finally; an experience I never had in middle school. My senior year was also marked by getting senior portraits, when photographers were called in to take a variety of pictures and poses of each senior student. Not meaning to brag, I really was the beautiful swan in high school. Even at my senior portraits, my photographers turned it into a modeling session with me and took three times as many pictures for free. To this day I look back and think, "wow, I was so pretty!" The photographers made me look absolutely exquisite. I was in several school clubs and organizations, again based on popularity, and it was just fun being a senior, especially considering I could do it "my way" without actually having to go to school too much. Teachers turned their heads when the "popular crowd" skipped, and as long as parents didn't find out, no harm no foul. Somehow I managed to graduate high school with a near overall 4.0 GPA, but I'll never know how, especially considering that I literally missed more days than I attended my senior year. To this day, that remains to be scolding joke in my family. At least we've been able to recover together enough to be able to make jokes about some of it because if you can't laugh about some things, you can't survive. It took many dangers to get there, but my family recovered with me, so I was never really as alone as I thought, and having recovered I know that now.

The momentum and adrenaline of my senior year kept me

manic enough to be happier than usual, but I still had several lows, self-destructive behaviors, and addictions as well. I failed a class, and had a strong vendetta with the teacher; to the point even, that she had me removed from her class and I was made a "helper" to the guidance advisor. Like that wasn't planned? I was still on all drugs, although I wasn't really concerned about it in a negative way. I had been dating a terrible man for over a year, and had no intentions of ending the relationship, regularly lied to my parents, and just overall didn't give a shit. I figured if there was ever time to screw up, it was now because I wasn't getting any younger. That was always my excuse when it came to things I did that were wrong. I fought everything and everyone. The school invoked a new no body piercings rule, so I chose the most obvious; a flashy tongue ring to show them how little I cared about their rules or my life. I was sent to the office several times, but I'd take the ring out for a few minutes then on the way to the office, so that by the time I got there (without the evidence in my mouth), what could the principals do? Ha! Ha! I thought!

My senior year was pivotal in two ways though; one, I felt that I was close enough to the edge of addiction for crack cocaine that I finally gave it up for good because I knew it was almost too late, and two I finally dumped the terrible man I had fallen in love with (well, the only love I had ever felt for a man regardless of whether it was real or not). Don't think that I made these decisions for the right reasons though because it still took many more years and disasters, many more twists and turns, many more battles and bumps in my road in my journey before I actually started making healthy decisions for the right reasons.

Memorable Moments

For as long as I can remember, my grandparents have always had some form of a garden. It always consisted of tomatoes, potatoes, carrots, and cucumbers, but in my childhood it had practically every imaginable vegetable and the garden took up a fourth of their very large yard. My granny was always the gardener, even though both my grandma and grandpa had their favorites too. I remember it all started with them.

My granny would take me out to the garden and we would search for the freshest to pick for dinner the next evening or for soon use thereafter. We always looked for "the good stuff" We walked together up and down her carefully planted and labeled rows, combing softly through leaves, and delicately stepping around all the beautiful forms of life in their various stages.

Paw, on the other hand, was the one I was able to be mischievous with. We didn't look for "the good (edible) stuff", we looked for "the bad stuff." I many remember many times that he had me laughing hysterically about rotten potatoes. The stories that he would tell and the jokes he would make about their stench would have me in fits of laughter until my stomach ached. Then the real fun began, we would sneak up on the other one and throw the rotten potatoes at each other. Mind you, I was probably four through eight in these years, so a thrown potato couldn't do that much harm, but we laughed our heads off about it for years.

Telling the Secrets

Always fearing honesty in other people's minds.
Believing in their cruelty and holding my secrets behind.
Crying out for help, but where do I begin?
I'm craving to be loved and cared for once again.
I expect to be hurt be because of my troublesome past.
Frightened down to tears; HOW LONG WILL MY PAIN
LAST?

Age 19

CHAPTER 14

My MENtal Status

It didn't take me long to realize that I hadn't been given a chance to "lose" my virginity because it had been "taken" from me. As a result I figured, screw it, I don't have anything special to give away anyways. Since this was my thought process, I threw away all of my preconceived notions about the "perfect first time" and just gave in and figured it didn't necessarily matter who or where anymore. I was already too damaged for it to matter, so why not fuck when a boyfriend asked? I didn't go through the years of wanting to, but resisting. I never had a boyfriend who I had to passionately struggle not to "go all the way" with. If I had a boyfriend, I just assumed early on that sex was part of a normal relationship. I wouldn't have dated the person if I didn't already have a guarantee in my mind that we would have sex. Yes, in some ways this made me a teenage whore but remember, I wasn't exactly someone who people were magnetically drawn to until my late high school years, so I didn't exactly have a lot of boyfriends. How was this impacted by my bipolar disorder and borderline personality tendencies? It is the high, the mania, the addiction to the control of sex. Sex was part of my illness, so it wasn't something that was impacted by it. Sex, in itself, was part of the illness. Overall my borderline personality tendencies made relationships very hard for me, and the unmedicated bipolar disorder was not a good combination for healthy relationships either.

I had premature crushes on boys for as long as I can remember. I always thought someone was cute, liked someone, or wanted to get someone's attention by showing off girly places that boys were supposed to like to see. I would bend over to try to attract a third grade boy's attention. Little did I know that they really didn't care until they got older anyways. Fourth grade was the biggest year of it for me, as far as my early development with boys was concerned because it was the year that I started making my crushes known, even if it meant asking a boy to be "my boyfriend." I wasn't to embarrassed or intimidated to ask, I just wanted the boyfriend I had a crush on. I repeated this cycle regularly even though we didn't officially do anything sexual.

The first boyfriend I had after I was released from the first treatment center was someone I had met in the treatment center. As an adult, I realize what a stupid decision that was; two teenagers with extreme issues getting together instead of attempting to at least be therapeutic, but I don't think either of us cared. That's about the same nonchalant attitude that I approached sex with. Why care? It didn't matter if I was happy, at least I was able to make someone else happy and temporarily feel good. Obviously the relationship didn't last. I needed very extensive treatment, as did he. I never knew enough about him to even guess at a his diagnosis, but he was really actually a scary person. Since I didn't care about life, I didn't realize it. As an adult, I realize that I had just taken one more dangerous opportunity. He was violent at times. I remember he actually pointed a gun at me, during what he considered role play before sex. I didn't care; we screwed anyways. The relationship would've never lasted, but my second hospital stay ended it immediately and we didn't talk again until nearly a decade later when we just happened to run into each other. Nothing came of it because I didn't want it too, but that's how it goes with small towns I guess. The ghosts are always there.

My next boyfriend was just for fun. I knew there would never be any love between us, but I was doing a lot of drugs at the time, and several of them boosted my mania even beyond its normal limits (if you can call any of mania "normal"). He wasn't even a boyfriend, just someone I called when I was at the top of the roller coaster. We were always able to find a place to stay and just fuck! Neither of us had to worry about parents walking in, and it was just the sensory release I needed when I felt the rise of mania. He was one of the original older guy friends that I had before I went to the hospital, so we didn't have to go through any of the formalities. We already knew each other, he hinted that he was attracted to me, and that's all it took. I wasn't one of those girls who had to hear "I love you" before romantically making love. I knew what my body was supposed to be used for. I had experiences already that taught me how men expected to be able to treat women, so I didn't mind succumbing to the raucousness of it. Our relationship, if you can call it that, lasted for many months. We never dated, we just called each other when we needed sex, but I was thrilled about that. It meant that someone liked me, needed me (even if it was only for my body) and kept coming back to me, so I must not be that crazy after all I figured! I learned that when you adjust your own expectations, anything can be acceptable, feel good, and feel like it helps.

My next boyfriend thought I was the best and sexiest woman in the world, but we were still young, and it never felt like "love" to me, even though I think it felt that way to him. He really did treat me right, and respect me in a way that I had never known. He was older, of course, and a friend of one of the guys I had known for so long now. He was just a kind, nice, caring, non-pushy, and romantic-hearted kind of guy. I hope he found his princess and is living happily ever after because he really was sweet enough to deserve it. Maybe that's why it never felt like love to me, because I never knew that was how a relationship was supposed to be. Actually, it didn't feel like love because it just wasn't. He was a great guy, but I didn't and just couldn't make myself fall in love with him, even after we had been together for a significant amount of time. I had the same theology though. We had sex early in the relationship, because again I figured, why not? That's just the way it was supposed to be, I knew. Besides my bipolar loved it! He was so nice, I shamefully took advantage because I was young and immature. When I was manic, with racing thoughts that felt scattered all over the place, he would just speed up with me. I'm sure he didn't mind me taking advantage of him for the sex though when I was manic, but he always understood my extra heightened sense of the need for it though. On the other hand, when I was significantly depressed and at the lowest of my lows, he tried to be as supportive as he could. I still wasn't diagnosed or correctly medicated, but he tried the best he could, and I do now really appreciate him for that.

As we parted, I was back to my typical need for the bad boy. This time, I choose nearly the worst. One who I could love and hate, and one who could love and hate me back. NOT at all good or healthy for a person with bipolar disorder. I was already on my own roller coaster, so it makes sense that adding another roller coaster in to the form of an unhealthy man was certainly not a good decision. Again though, I was still somewhat suicidal in some moods, and undiagnosed. I had finally given up on my prescribed medications altogether and just self medicated through drugs. These were some of the years I described in my high school years. As big of a supporter as I wanted my family to be, they weren't. I wanted them to support our relationship and realize that he really was a good guy, and they didn't. My immaturity made me feel like they were unsupportive of me, but in reality, they were supportive of me, just not him (for very good reasons). This was a brick wall between me and my family, and I just retreated. I loved him, so screw them. He loved me, so their opinions didn't matter. Now medicated and correctly diagnosed, I ponder, what the hell was I thinking?!?!

Our relationship lasted for nearly two years, but it was only my view of what our relationship was. We can trick our mind into believing anything, cant we? The borderline in me loved it because I could be happy as long as I believed what we were, and my mind really believed it. All of the thoughts I had about our relationship I really believed. It wasn't as if I was trying to cover up for him, or make excuses. It was just truly what I believed. I believed he loved me. I believed we were monogamous. I believed we would marry and live happily ever after. I believed that he was telling the truth 100% of the time. Sometimes I knew better, but I still honestly believed that all was right with him nearly all the times. This was probably one of the most unhealthiest relationships I ever had, as far as my bipolar disorder and borderline personality tendencies was concerned because he was as unpredictable as I was. The more his roller coaster fluctuated, the more mine seemed triggered. He also encouraged my borderline personality tendencies because his nature was the same. It was easier for me to go back and forth when the person I was dating seemed to do the same thing. He never seemed to pick up on any of my instabilities because he was as unstable as I was, so the drugs, mental illnesses, and personality switches were too easy and common place between us. Definitely not a good relationship.

Now, I know what you're thinking, all women have been surprised at some point or another about an act committed by a significant other. This was different though, only in that it was touched so drastically by mental illness. When the borderline in me took over, I believed what I really thought I saw. It seemed like this occurred more frequently as I reached mania. When the other side of the borderline took over and I had minor glimpses of what my reality really was, it only led to the bottom of my roller coaster. The combination of my array of diagnosis nearly killed me yet again. Drugs, attempts to overdose, cutting, skipping school, running away, refusing to come home; I did everything every impulse I had led me to do without so much as a second thought. It took a "coming to Jesus" talk with a really kind hearted friend to nudge me out of that relationship. Broken hearted, and mentally fucked up, I ended it and rebounded with the man who would eventually become my husband. The only one night stand I had ever had up to this point, and it led to my marriage.

Ironically enough, this good friend, was also someone I looked for and successfully found after my divorce. For the same reason I always looked for men. Sex is always the answer. Surprising, and embarrassingly enough, I offered as usual, and he stopped me because he wanted to wait so we could be a serious relationship. Immediately I was swept off my feet, and practically in love, just after hearing those words. This part of my life ended being excruciatingly painful because we did both, make love and have wild sex, but my heart was involved and broken. Nonetheless, it was just one more habit of mania that I initiated and tried to follow through on. In the end, rather it was due to mental illness or not, my heart was broken and I hurt within the pit of my soul again.

Memorable Moments

Even though most of my life was influenced by tragedies or mental illnesses, I am so thankful and fortunate to have the family that I do. My family may not have always understood me, but they are the most wonderful, loving, and supportive group of people I have ever known. Everyone…my parents, grandparents, extended family, truly everyone has been able to accept me for who I am. Now that I have found the right treatment and medications I'm sure, from their perspective, I am a lot easier to deal with, even though I still may not be easy. Even in my toughest years though, they never gave up on me.

I have unique memories with all of them. My grandma and I spend our time, when we can, going on brief shopping trips. My paw and I share our love for music, so I pull my truck up to his back porch, turn my speakers up as loud as I can, and let him float away of the songs the same way that I do. My aunt is my rock who helps guide me through some of the tough times. I trust her with my soul, and only wish that everyone could have someone so important and special to them in their lives. My mom is my love who will also care, support, and love me no matter who I am, and no matter what mistakes I have made or will make. She has always tried her best to help me, and show me unconditional love. My dad and my brother were my protectors who stood strong when I felt weak. Again, I reiterate, how lucky can a girl get to have so many wonderful people involved in her life?

Alone

Why don't you ask me my secrets and fears?
Why don't you ask me the cause of my tears?
Do you not care enough to know?
How I'm feeling inside when my real pain is shown?
I feel betrayed, forgotten, and all alone,
but I can't let my feelings on the inside be known.
I keep running from a fear that I cannot see.
I've cried out for help, but no one can save me.
I wish I understood what I keep trying to hide.
But no matter what, I have to keep them tucked

deep

down

inside.

Age 21

CHAPTER 15

College Bound?

Although I had different opportunities after graduating from high school, I knew that college was the only thing for me...if I could survive until then, but I wouldn't have cared if I didn't. Nonetheless, my reason for college was simple. It was the only way I could get to do the work that I wanted to do for as long as I had to continue living. During mania, I would send applications to the more prestigious colleges, knowing full well that I would stay at the local colleges. I just wanted the reminder of how smart I was. There was just never any doubt in my mind that I would attend college. If I was alive still at the time, I knew I would go to college. Even through the worst years when I was either hooked to drugs, when I expelled or at risk of being expelled, I still just somehow knew in the back of my mind that I would go to college. Only if I couldn't kill myself first, that is. Moreover, I knew exactly what I was going to get my degrees in too, so at least I had a back up plan. That also gave me a glimmer of optimism with hope and life, even though I didn't know it at the time.

I rejoiced my high school graduation because it certified my adulthood (as much as I could until I was twenty-one). My family probably just celebrated the fact that I had graduated at all though because I had driven them all through hell and back to finish high school, actually my whole life probably. Either way it was a very positive celebration and one where the excitement of it all triggered me strait to mania days before the actual ceremony. I was calling my best friend relentlessly about what to wear, make up, parties afterwards, drinking, guys, how much trouble I couldn't wait to get into when it was all said and done; not at all the typical stuff "normal" teenagers do after graduation but I somehow managed to always take it one step further. If one mental illness didn't get in the way, another did. When one mental illness crept in, it always invited company too.

Even though my mania began before my graduation, I was actually on a descent by the time the actual ceremony came. I regret it now, even though I couldn't necessarily control my moods, because I even look angry in several of the pictures that I had taken with my family that night. One moment I was animatedly walking and talking to my best friend through the parking lot draping ribbons from all of my various club involvements over my shoulders, and the next minute I was pissed that the "helpers" kept readjusting my hair, gown, and ribbons. Just leave me the hell alone, I thought. I couldn't help it. What had started as a cycle that seemed like it was going to swing for days, turned into a cycle that was going to swing for hours and for days even too. I couldn't just celebrate and be happy.

A few days after graduation, I celebrated by getting drunk and doing drugs with my best friend and then with the terrible boyfriend I'd had for nearly two years of high school. He was either a sweetheart drunk or a maniac raging drunk (and you never knew which it would be) so our "celebrations" were always eventful. This particular night, his drunkenness turned into rage.

He screamed, threw things, shattered glass, nearly destroyed the contents of more than one room while I just sat there numbly smoking pot. I wasn't even scared. Part of me hoped that his rage would cause my accidental death. When it didn't and the drunken smoothness finally settled in, we laughed about it, smoked some more pot, fucked, and he settled into a drunken stupor sleep.

Later that night and into the early hours the next morning I sat in the bathroom and cried because I knew that I finally had to kill myself, but I was frustrated because I couldn't figure out a surefire way to do it. The major mood depressive disorder, bipolar, borderline, and anxiety were just too much. I just couldn't do it anymore. I couldn't understand that the reason my life was so horrible was because of the choices I made; I saw no direct link. Suicide shouldn't be so hard, I thought. Even though I was completely wasted, I thought I definitely had a chance since my boyfriend was passed out, my family couldn't find me if they tried, and his roommates wouldn't be home for hours. Perfect timing, I thought. Taking into consideration I was drunk and drugged beyond oblivion, it was pretty amazing that I was even aware enough to figure all this out.

I picked the up the biggest pieces of glass and set them aside to be used for later. I searched the contents of their medicine cabinet, but didn't even find a vitamin. I couldn't believe they didn't have anything. I finally started searching his roommate's rooms when I found a bottle of Tylenol. Bingo! A splintered glass as sharp as razor blades from broken beer bottles, and the deadly combinations of drugs, booze, and pills. I can't possible fail this time! I didn't even hesitate or bother to cover up the evidence that I had been in my boyfriend's roommate's rooms. I ran back to the bathroom, rushed inside, locked the door, and sat against it to spend my last few minutes on earth in silent reflection.

I don't know how long I sat there, but I had been going back and forth between all my favorite liquors, so time was the last thing I cared about, It was all the same to me on a night like this. Graduation was such an overload to me that I quickly shot into mania, and rapidly dropped (not even fell) to the floor of the roller coaster. I swallowed all of the Tylenol pills with every drink I had; this had to be enough, I thought, even though his bottle only contained 9 pills left. When I began to feel drowsy from the pills and drinks, I kept myself awake by slashing my wrists as hard as I could. I had even heard an old wives tale in one of my hospital stays (don't know if it's true or not) that after you slashed your wrist you should put it in the toilet and flush because the suction would further draw your blood out. Of course I even did this too. I was ready to die. Happy to die. And happy this was it. I would be gone.

Whoever knows how many hours later, my boyfriend's roommate's girlfriend was scooping me up off the ground and helping me into the shower. She didn't even try to get my clothes off. I think I was so close to death that she just wanted to climb in with me to be sure that I stayed alive, which is exactly what she did. She didn't ask any questions, and I didn't offer and answers. I couldn't have talked anyways. How I survived this attempt I'll never know, other than timing. If she would've been five, ten, thirty, sixty minutes later, it might have been too late. I didn't want to get caught and have this suicide attempt foiled like all of the others had been, but when I look at where I am at now, I'm glad that it was interrupted. I felt horribly ill for several days, and even passed out briefly a few times (even once at the public mall to make matters worse), but yet again it was another unsuccessful attempt, so I guess I was going to college after all. It was time to get serious in one direction or the other.

I stayed to attend the local college, truth be told, because I had envisioned the terrible boyfriend and I living happily ever after. This was near the end of our relationship though. Ironically enough though, part of me knew this was never a possibility because I knew he was wrong for me on so many different levels, but the borderline in me loved it because in certain moods I could identify with every word out of his mouth. He told outrageous and unbelievable lies. Everyone knew they were lies because they were too unbelievable to be true, but it didn't stop him from trying to convince people. I could believe it though, and even did the same thing. That's what borderline feels like. You may tell outrageous lies or have such a different personality, but its not by choice. It is a realistic belief!

I broke up with the boyfriend, and had my one night stand rebound at the beginning of my first semester as a college freshman. As I explained earlier, one of my friends had a heart to heart conversation with me about that relationship so I knew it had to end, no matter how painful it would be. I wasn't looking for love and didn't even give a damn if I found it. I just wanted to lessen the pain of a break up in the only way I knew how; rebound! I went on a double date with my best friend and her boyfriend, and a friend of theirs that I had recently met. We had a really fun great time, and went to a really nice place, but I was so manic in pushing myself to get over my last boyfriend that he could've just taken me for a burger and soda and I would've fucked him anyways. That's just how I did things, even though I had never had a one night stand before with a man I hadn't known. We all drank with our meals, came back to my friends house, and went to our separate rooms for our time to get nasty and naked! I got exactly what I wanted and then quickly left. It was the perfect excuse to leave after good sex, but I really did have to get back home. Believe it or not, I did really have a curfew when that part of my personality chose to obey it. I left a note saying thanks under the wiper of his windshield, and then just left.

"You don't have to do this," I said the next day when he called. "I really like you (I said, knowing full well that I didn't even really know him) but you don't have to do this," I insisted. He said that he called because he wanted to, and that he had enjoyed our time together. I agreed that it was great, and from then on we started planning more dates. We were limited on time though because he would be leaving within two weeks for a month long training for his career. After the training, he would not even have a choice in his living location, so it was a relationship neither of us expected to go very far. We enjoyed it for the time we had though. We went to lunch. Had sex. Went to dinner. Had sex. Went to walk along the water's edge at the park. Had sex. It was a great few weeks that I enjoyed, but in mania, I enjoyed it even more. Sometimes it just happens that way. A good time can be greatened by mania or ruined by the depths or a crash. You just never know!

He kept calling though, and I kept looking forward to his calls. One month later, I was flying to see him at his training location. I remember we went to a nice dinner the first night that I got there. We had already had a few drinks, but neither of us was drunk. This was the time and place where I first told him that I loved him. "Don't say it until you mean it though, but I just wanted to tell you," I added. Later that night after we made love was the first time he told me that he loved me too. Over the next few days we just couldn't get enough of each other. We did as much as we could, we talked until the early morning hours of dawn, we wined and dined at the best places in town. It was a great reunion getting to see him again, but we still didn't know if he would end up working close enough to my hometown for us to build a relationship or not. I don't know where I was on my roller coaster, but it must have been traveling somewhat smoothly at the time because I felt as stable as I possibly could. Rebounding successfully and easily kept me happy, but having such strong feelings for him living elsewhere kept me realistic, so I was numbly happy somewhere in between.

Then finally the news! He would be somewhere where we could still continue our relationship without his job interfering too much! I saved every souvenir from our time together; receipts, napkins, hotel amenities, everything that served as a reminder of him. A week later though the major mood depressive disorder and the depths of bipolar had invaded me yet again. I was ready for suicide because I knew he was Romeo and I was Juliet and that we could never really happy to be together because I was just to screwed up, and one day he would be able to tell. By the time I got home from the week visit I had with him I was manic again.

Altogether we dated for five years. In this time, we pretended to be normal even though we each had our own obvious problems. The longer we dated, the more I realized that his drinking wasn't a "casual thing". I don't know if he ever picked up on the fact that I suffered from several mental illnesses, even in the years we were married too, but he knew there was something off-key about me too, I'm sure. Because his drinking was such a problem for him, I quit drinking completely in hopes that he would also decide not to drink anymore. Besides, I was helping to raise his daughter Noel; a responsibility I took very seriously!

Our relationship was an important turning point in my life, not only because I was very serious about college, but also because I took my job being involved in Noel's life very seriously. I always helped to be sure that she had enough healthy food, brushed her teeth, and had nice clean clothes to wear. We had fun picking out books and toys together. Noel was a great kid, and helped me remember the importance of my disguise even more. I just had to hide the moods as much as possible because Noel was involved too. It wasn't just me anymore. Even though Ryan and I were only dating, I took my relationship with Noel very seriously. However important this time and change of my life may have been, it still just wasn't enough though. I was able to do better as long as I smoked pot constantly, but I still knew that I had a long way to go before I was ever really "right." I just accepted that I never would be.

I proved to be a natural at college though. Don't get me wrong, I had my fair share of classes that I struggled with, but I made great grades, had a good rapport with my instructors, and generally excelled. I loved reading, and found out that I also loved learning about the passion that would become my career. It wasn't something that I just did. It was something that I loved. I was thrilled at that, but also scared to death. I had finally seemed to have everything – a boyfriend, a college schedule that would lead me to a career that I would love, a child that would be my stepdaughter who was as perfect as a spring day – but I still couldn't stop the roller coaster or personalities. I sailed through my A.A. degree and then decided to take a year off before beginning my long haul to what I had planned (getting my bachelors and Masters degrees).

The year I was away from college, I earned a living stipend for completing more than two thousand volunteer hours. I worked at various schools with students who were considered to be at risk. I absolutely loved it because I *understood* them. I had *felt* the same way…and sometimes still did (even though I would never admit that to students). When they talked, I listened and tried to help them as realistically as I could. I wanted them to know that I genuinely cared and loved them, and that their safety was important to me. It was almost a perfect medication for me. Whenever I was feeling low, I could remind myself how much I was helping others and it would help somewhat. The problem was though that it never stopped me from getting too low. Nothing could stop the lows anymore than it could stop the highs.

During this year of volunteering, I had a variety of jobs to help diverse members of the community. One of these assignments placed me within the realm of a police officer whose duty was to protect younger children. Without going into the specific details of time and place, this officer cornered me and proceeded to sexually harass me. I can't say I was shocked by the molestation that had occurred when I was four because I didn't fully understand that it was wrong at that age. I can't even say that the rape shocked me because for years I felt guilt because I had purposefully put myself in bad positions. This incident though with the police officer, shocked the hell out of me. Think about it for a moment. What do we teach our kids? If you ever need help, get an adult or police officer, right? Well I was barely an adult myself at twenty, and he proceeded to tell me every vulgar thought, memory, and inclination that he had. I only asked him to stop twice because I had known from experience that the words "stop" and "no" meant absolutely nothing, so I just stood cornered by him numbly listening to a man old enough to be my grandfather describe all the sexual actions and positions he could think of, desired, had seen, or previously tried.

I went home on my lunch break and told Ryan. Even though we weren't married yet, we lived together for years prior to our marriage. He was as freaked out by it as I was. I returned to work and talked to a trusted friend there about it. He insisted that I tell someone on a higher level about it. Nearing hysterics, I did just that. I was so humiliated. It was horrifically embarrassing to have to retell these kinds of things, yet one more time in my life. The last thing I said before leaving my superior's office was, "who would've ever imagined that he would do something like this?" I'll never forget my superior's answer, "we all did. We were just waiting for it to happen to someone."

Go figure, we know he's a pervert, but let's go ahead and hire him anyways at the expense of causing emotional grief to someone else! As long as it isn't your problem, you don't have to be the one who fixes it or attempts to heal from it. Obviously there was an investigation, but it didn't go very far because the officer finally got caught in enough lies, and admitted to it all. When the sheriff asked what I would hope for out of his charges, my only response was "that he never be allowed to work around children again." I didn't care if he went to jail or not, but I didn't ever want him to be in the position of hurting a little girl like I had been hurt so badly so many times when I was younger. I had been through the process of pressing charges against a perpetrator. I didn't want any part of it ever again, but protecting other children from experiences similar to mine was very important to me. Since there was no helping me, I at least wanted to help them. Within a week, my home was broken into by the police officer and the sheriff himself came to help me move my family to a more secure and unknown location.

As far as college goes, when my year of volunteering was finished, I eagerly jumped back in. As boring as college was, I liked the feelings it gave me when I did so well. In less than four years I completed both my bachelors and masters degrees, despite having to commute an hour and a half both ways. I knew what career I was meant for, so I went at it with all my might! I didn't have a college graduation party because my life was as normal as I could make it at this time. I was still off the walls borderline, bipolar, and anxious, but I had enough adult strategies to hide it...most, actually maybe only some of the time. I enjoyed this accomplishment with my family. I look back in the past, and I wouldn't have wanted it any other way. I thought, "I FINALLY DID IT!" Wrong! Yes, I finally got the degrees, but I should've been more specific in my victory. Completing college and earning degrees still wasn't enough to protect me from mental illness and keep me sane.

"With age comes wisdom," the saying declares. Well, I also must add that with age comes more strategies. From the time I first started having the inklings of mental illness, even before I knew what mental illness was, I already had some ingrained strategies on how to disguise it. The older I got, I developed strategies to cover up my true self based on what I saw out of my peers. Therefore, I learned from and mimicked the actions of my peers in the hospitals too. Finally, as an adult, I felt that I had perfected my strategies that I could live with the illness as long as I could keep up the charades of disguises. Now I had the degrees to prove that I could. But I gave up, and let go again.

Memorable Moments

Every visit to my aunt and uncle's house was fun. I knew that if I was going to their house, it was a guarantee that I would have a blast. First of all, they always had the coolest house in the world. They had a pool – a must have for a house that qualified as cool for youngsters. They also had a Jacuzzi, a pool table, a bird avery, a game room, and every toy possibly imaginable since my cousin stayed there on occasion. It was a kid's paradise! Although every time was wondrous, one time that sticks out in my mind specifically was the night I spent the night and we made homemade candles! At the time, it was the most interesting idea I had ever heard of, and I was ecstatic about making one with my aunt and cousin.

I must admit, my aunt always had the most fun and creative ideas, and she still does. As a child and adult, I am always amazed at what she knows. My cousin and I each chose a color we wanted our candle to be and had to pick as many of those colors out of the crayon box as we could. My cousin chose blue, and peeled the wrappers off various blue crayons. I had a hard time deciding between red and purple, but in the end, purple won and I started scraping the wrapping off all the purplish crayons. The trick was to melt the wax, pout it into a container, put ice cubes into it to make designs as it hardened, and put in the refrigerator overnight. Although the process took quite a while, it was definitely well worth it. Our candles both turned our very special and beautiful.

Broken, Damaged, and Hoping for Death

I give you all I have.
You then take it away.
I lay upon a slab
waiting for the day
that I can feel somewhat happy
and hold my head up high
to be a normal child and never wish to die.
To wish to never cut.
To be cured of dangerous thoughts,
but no, I'm bound by chains
of suffering, pain, and loss.
I have no friends who care for me
and very little hope.
I seem to be quite short the skills
that it takes for me to cope.

Age 14

CHAPTER 16

Loving, But Having To Leave

$\mathcal{I}$t was Christmas Day when Ryan proposed. Everyone knew that he was going to, but me. Of course, I had hoped that he would, but sometimes you can't ever be quite sure of when to expect a proposal. He had talked to his family and Noel about it, he had asked for my parents permission and blessing, and purchased a beautiful ring. On Christmas morning, since we had Noel and she was still young, it was as hectic as any Christmas is with any child. We had all opened our presents, and were happily going through our new gifts. Ryan kept looking for one last gift he had for me, and finally found it at the back of the Christmas tree. It was wrapped and named for me. I tore open the wrapper and found a cracker jack box. He prompted me about what was inside a cracker jack box with the cracker jacks…a prize. I tore the box open, carefully opened the wrapper to the prize packet, and found my engagement ring. Immediately and happily I said yes.

Although I was skeptical of getting married for the obvious reasons I explained earlier, I was also excited to get to be the princess bride that I always wanted to be. Everything just had a magical beauty to it, and it was, exactly the wedding I had always dreamed of. It was the most beautiful day of my entire life, and it moved so quickly that I didn't even have time to stop and think if I was on top, in the middle, or at the bottom of the roller coaster. I was one semester shy of graduating, loved the little girl who would become my stepdaughter (Noel), and honestly thought Ryan and I could fix things together. Love is a powerful thing, but even love isn't enough sometimes.

Ryan and I weren't stupid, we knew we had problems, but we loved each other enough that we had every confidence that things would work out very well in the end. We gave it our best effort too, but his job allowed us to be apart for days every week, and I don't think that helped to straighten out an already somewhat troubled marriage. Not that I blame him, he was a provider, but it made communication even more difficult. My undiagnosed, unmedicated, and untreated mental illnesses didn't make matters any easier though either.

Bipolar or not, divorced or not, we did have a lot of good times too though. Giving credit when credit is due, for a while we were both happy (for me, always impacted by mental illness so I may not have always appeared to be happy). We took dancing lessons together, took family vacations, had family snowball fights, and just loved being together. We used to hide messages for each other in funny places like the microwave or by the toothbrushes that said, "I love you," "have a great day." Moments like that I treasure, and will never forget.

Once we even had to get rid of a mattress when we were living in a two story house, and like mischievous children, we took turns sliding down the stairwell on the mattress. We would drag it up the stairs and laugh all the way down as we slid down on the mattress without a care in the world. We were happy for a long time, and I can easily admit to that. Other times we picked on each other as a joke. We took turns secretly trying to sneak up on each other in the shower. Not in a sexual way either, although we did have our fair share of that too. One of us would creep up on the other while the other was in the shower. Whoever the creeper was would dump a huge cup of ice cold water on the unexpected bather. That trick gave us many laughs over the years

When he was in town, we worked as a team to raise Noel through doctors, dentists, school, and extracurricular activities. We all had a good time with it, but no matter what I ever did, it was never enough to just stop my roller coaster. As ashamed as I am to admit it, I was still self medicating with marijuana up until the point when I *had* to quit (when I adopted my Taylor for fear of random testing).

Ryan's drinking had been a big problem before the marriage, but I was in love, young, naïve, and didn't know enough about alcoholism. Even though we were a happy family at times too, there were still times she and I had to "go eat at McDonalds and go play by ourselves for a while" so Noel wouldn't see the rage her daddy caused because he was at home drunk. I knew it was a problem, but still wasn't completely aware of what it would lead to. I cannot say that bipolar moods are always due to a specific trigger. A lot of the times, it is just a natural part of our lives regardless of circumstances. Sensory overloads or circumstances, among other things, can cause a high or low or even a speed up of emotions though we run the bipolar race. These escapes from Ryan sometimes could be a trigger to my bipolar disorder that sped up my roller coaster.

Although Ryan and I always had a very troubled marriage, I continued to hope that we could fix things for a long time. I know he thought we could too, otherwise we would've parted ways sooner. Ryan's drinking was a huge problem. My over zealous ambitions and raving energy were huge problems, not to mention my mental illness. We had issues to work on, to say the least, but we also had a lot of fun. We continued to travel whenever we could, we bought pets, we bought used furniture and things to fix our home with…we just had fun.

We had birds that we use to laugh about when they teasingly pecked at each other when they were standing on the doors of our entertainment unit. We had two cats, and Noel was too young to say his shelter name – Siam, so we all named him kitty. Then we got our second cat when we got Taylor, and he couldn't say her name, so he named her "Tray Bird." Who knows why? We did have many wonderful times though, despite the divorce. I must not have been an easy unmedicated wife, but we did have our fair share of good times. His inner demons seemed to be all related to addictions, whereas mine were mental illnesses. Neither of us even had a chance of beating our flaws without extensive help. I accepted my flaws and will always be certain to get the help and treatment I need, whereas he still hasn't accepted his flaws or the need for help. Individually, or together, we were untreatable. I don't blame the crumble of our marriage on that, but that's how I felt for a long time.

Essentially our marriage didn't crumble, it shattered the year I adopted Taylor and gave birth to Anna. All within that year we became damaged beyond repair because a mother hen will always feel more drawn to protect her chicks than anything else, and I became the only unaddicted parent; the defensive and protective mother hen. Not that I was perfect, by any stretch of the imagination, but I had total confidence that my actions would never harm the children. I didn't, and never would have, that confidence with him because of his drinking. No matter how much of a friendship we would be able to develop in the future (as we have) I wouldn't be able to have the trust that he would refrain from drinking around the kids. I couldn't trust that he would not put them in harms way again as he had in the past.

However, my children are the best things that ever happened to me. Well, that and a diagnosis and medications that actually work. Taylor was originally my nephew on Ryan's side of the family. He was born while Ryan and I were on our honeymoon, so we weren't there for Taylor's actual birth. When his mother was pregnant, we anticipated problems because she already had other children from a previous marriage who were experiencing difficulties, and she had already proven to be a poor mother, but I had no idea it would go as far as it did.

To leave Taylor with his own privacy, I will omit the experiences my son had to endure prior to coming to live with us. I can say that it didn't help my moods any. As a bipolar, again, I'm already prone to mood swings. Throw in an extra factor such as gambling with a child (which is what it felt like) and the mood swings are that much more frequent, in depth, and widespread. I was so determined to get him because I knew how much we needed each other, and I had personally witnessed how bad off he was and how much worse it was getting. It only felt like a gamble because at times we knew that we were going to positively be able to adopt him, but due to the system, at other times we weren't so sure so that instability wrecked havoc on my already mentally ill nerves!

Our daughter Anna was just as much as a surprise as Taylor was, except that she was not adopted. Since our marriage was rapidly deteriorating, it wasn't too hard to pinpoint the date…the anniversary of the day we met. My pregnancy with Anna was so easy and normal. I was thrilled about having a girl and became obsessed with pink. I loved feeling her kick and hiccup, or turn in somersaults. Sometimes it felt like she was bigger than I was because she was so active. The labor and delivery were hard, but a million times worth it. She was born perfect! Slightly jaundiced, but a beautiful 6.5 oz bundle of preciousness. Anna looked just like me too, so that was so amazing to see. She was just a little princess from the very beginning. Dressed in a newborn dress that was way too big for her, we brought her home and got some preemie clothes. She wore preemies until she was nearly two months. Anna's tiny size wasn't because she was sick or anything, she was just petite. Her smallness made me want to keep her that much closer to me to protect her from the world too.

After Anna was born, and after Ryan was fired and did not even attempt to complete the drug and alcohol program, I was finally prepared for the divorce. As I said earlier, my family helped (and annoyed me!), moved me out, and cleaned up and restored the house Ryan and I owned to be sold. I scrounged up the money for an attorney start on the divorce papers as soon as possible. It was finally time to focus on fixing me! I started at my general practitioners office; I trusted her and she knew my history. She said I was suffering from depression, due to the obvious circumstances, and prescribed me with an anti-depressant and a short and immediate acting anti-anxiety medication.

While this would've worked for a typical individual suffering from circumstantial depression and anxiety, it is a very dangerous combination for a person with bipolar disorder. My general practitioner wasn't wrong, I was going through circumstantial problems that at time seemed insurmountable. It is understandable that this could lead to depression. She wouldn't have been able to diagnose me as bipolar, and it took several months before she recommended that I go to a specialist of psychology (only because she had prescribed so much and the problem didn't seem to be going away). In other words, I took two medications for nearly a year before my mind finally gave up and collapsed altogether and she recognized my freefalling and directed me to get help.

My children were always my one and only driving force through it all though, so even though I still seemed to be "beating my head against a brick wall" as far as getting the help I needed was concerned, that didn't deter my dedication to "fixing" myself though. They needed me. I was all they had, and that kept me going…most of the time. Did my mental illnesses win in the end? In some ways, yes, and in some ways no. As Anna aged, it was as wondrous as it was with my Taylor, except that I didn't get to enjoy him until he was a little older. It just amazes me, in general, to watch children grow, and my beautiful and perfect babies were, and always will be, the center or my heart, soul, and life. Unmedicated though, yes my mental illness won, and I just gave up on the hope that I could ever really been "fixed." I was trying and trying and trying to get myself the right kind of help, regardless of what it was, but I just couldn't seem to find it. I just figured it was because I was plainly just too fucked up. That's a hard thought to accept when you know that it means that your children will suffer as a result of you.

Memorable Moments

My honeymoon with Ryan was magical. I was Cinderella and he was my prince. When we boarded he carried me into our cabin; our threshold. In the good times (and bad times towards the end of our marriage) I will always positively remember the great time we had together on this trip and other occasions, and the strength of love that we felt for each other. It was the best of the best. We were in love, newly married, and loved every moment of being inseparable on the trip.

Our trip ported at Jamaica, Grand Cayman, and Mexico, but we could've stayed on the boat and had just as much fun just being together. We were in love. We were happy. We were broke, but browsed the gift shops anyways. We went on the cheapest excursions on shore, and felt the magic together as we tightly held hands or snuggled and learned into each other. In Jamaica, he took pictures of me as I had my hair braided, and I walked with him when we were walking along the market type of set ups. In Grand Caymen, we toured the area and swam with the sting rays. What an amazing feeling! The waist length water, and the silvery rays gliding through the water. We learned exactly how to feed them scooping the squid and squishing it at the top of our curled hand.

We giggled, took pictures, and fell even more in love with each other just because it was us and we were having fun. In Mexico we went to seven mile beach break. We held hands as we walked along the long shoreline. We cozily settled into our own space, picnicked, and made love there tucked away on the shore of the most beautiful beach you could ever see. The entire trip was crammed full of beautiful moments and memories for me.

Letting Go

I'm sitting here thinking of you
as my eyes well up with tears.
I'm thinking of you just the same
and remembering how you calmed my fears.
I remember how you dried my eyes.
I remember how you calmed me down.
I remember all your loving hugs.
I knew you'd always be around.
I knew you'd be there everyday.
I knew you'd be there by my side.
I knew you'd be there to catch my tears.
I knew you'd be there so see me cry.
You knew the times that I needed you there.
You knew the times I needed a friend.
You knew deep down when I was scared inside.
I thought those feelings would never end.

Age   19

CHAPTER 17

Any Offers On The House?

The house sat on the market for months without selling. We lowered the prices and finished fixing it up and doing everything we could to make it more appealing. It was just a tough market to try to sell a house in. Already the price we were asking was less that the actual amount we owed, but I just wanted out. Out of my commitment to the house. Out of my commitment to Ryan. I just wanted OUT! It felt like the harder I tried, the more he resisted or avoided. True or not, I don't know, but it pissed me the hell off that I was struggling my ass off to raise two kids right and trying to maintain them in a safe home and he was so nonchalant about everything. I had sworn not to ever to back into "The House of Adultery and Sin," after cleaning up his condoms and I didn't, but his carefree attitude towards it, and seemingly the kids, was finally the "straw that broke the camels back." It was the knife that pierced my heart because it was finally what led me to hit my bottom.

I tried to have a conversation with Ryan with both of our mothers present to discuss the hopeful sale of the house, and how we felt that he had been avoiding his share of work and payments. His attitude was very nonchalant and uncaring. My mom did most of the talking about the house, because at this point, I didn't give a shit about the house. After my mom realized we were getting no where with the discussion of the house, my mom asked, "well, what about the kids? You have obligations to them?" "Fuck the kids," he said. "I don't give a shit about them either." My mom stiffly retorted, "Well, you have financial obligations, and when you don't meet those obligations, I have to and that isn't right either." I could tell she was angered, but she did such a great job remaining calm through it all. He evilly turned to her and said, "well, then I hope you enjoyed the wild, fucking ride!" I SNAPPED! I just couldn't handle hearing my kids AND my mom spoken so harshly of, so I just came unglued. I jumped up and beat the shit out of my soon-to-be ex husband right there in front of both of our moms. The bipolar disorder had been manically and angrily building up, so I can't say that I was surprised by my actions. The only justification I have is on the moral basis that I cant stand by and listen to someone talk about my mama and children like that!

An hour later, I was picked up by the police for domestic violence. Since the kids weren't present when it occurred or even aware of it, I wasn't a risk to the Department of Children and Families. Nonetheless, the only night my children have ever spent away from me was the night I spent in jail. THAT is the beginning of what made me change. I was handcuffed and led from my home in the back of a squad car. From there I was finger printed, had mug shots taken, and was led to a holding cell with shackles and handcuffs. Hours later, I was transferred to the jail and placed within a cell by myself for another few hours until they processed me. Finally I was transferred to a cell of several other women who were recent inmates. New inmates started in the same cells until they knew that we could handle being moved to a more long term cell placement. I was only in jail for less than twenty-four hours, but I did a tremendous amount of soul searching in that time. I was so overwhelmed that I went through both mania and the lows. I felt shattered and fell apart. I screamed at my mom when I was allowed to make phone calls. I worried sick that my children were missing me. I was pissed at the guards just because I needed someone to hate. AND I KNEW that I may not fit in anywhere in the world, but I certainly didn't fit in jail. I knew then and there that I was meant for more, and had to do something to get myself on the right track for good.

Spending a night in jail showed me so many things. It showed me the sadness in the other mother's eyes who were already condemned to being there much longer. Since the cells don't exactly offer privacy, we were all able to hear them sobbing when they got off the phone with their children. Others were angry at their family members or boyfriends for getting them in trouble or refusing to bail them out, so we heard the screaming matches from their end of the conversation. Some were scared, and so we were able to hear the fear in their voices, and then there were the others like me who tried to disappear and just be numb.

Many of the women talked about the other times they were arrested and their other previous experiences. It embarrassed me that this was my second experience with a judge; the first being when I adopted my son. What a difference! My life had finally spiraled far enough that I knew it would kill me if I didn't fix it. In the past, this wouldn't have bothered me, but now I was mommy to two kids who didn't have anyone else. I finally had enough reasons to do for myself and my family what I should have done years earlier. Not that I didn't try in therapy or in the hospitals, but I should've been more persistent as I got older, and now it was time to start making demands about my mental health.

In the end, the charges were dropped because it was really a pretty simple, cut and dry case, without any hard core evidence that I had done anything terribly wrong. Regardless, I was ready to scream for help OUT LOUD if that's what it took. Never again would I be away from my children because I couldn't hold my emotions together. Never!

Memorable Moments

My favorite competition ever was the one I consider the most important. In high school I had a qualifying time that put me in the fastest category in the state, so along with the other elite swimmers in my district, I traveled to race at State. As soon as I walked into the International Swimming Hall of Fame pool, I felt goosebumps. It was a multi layered facility as big as the Olympics training pools. I was ecstatic to be these, especially considering how I got there.

It was a typical morning at 3:30 a.m. and I was blissfully sleeping. Suddenly I was jarred from my sleep as my phone by my bed started loudly ringing. I grabbed it quickly and mumbled a groggy, "hello." Swim season had just ended a week ago at the district competition, and since I didn't make it to state, it had a few extra hours of sleep and was surprised to be woken up. It was my best friend who was on the swim team. "Guess what?" she practically yelled! "You made it too! Your going to state! They took the next fastest time because someone else disqualified, so your going! Were at practice now, so come because we are all so excited!" I hung up, raced into my moms room with stumbly legs because I was so excited, threw her door open, and yelled, "I did it mom! I made it to state!" I was so happy that I cried the entire way to practice at 4:30 in the morning!

The pool facility, trip, family support, team camaraderie, and the entire experience in general was one of the best memories ever. Since I was a teenager, I have thousands of pictures to prove it because we took the silliest pictures of everything!

Friends, Enemies, or Family?

They speak of the truth, which she cannot hear.
They wade within shadows and wait within fear.
Inside she's a child who's secretly scared
She's afraid of the pain she alone cannot bear
She pictures a family and people who care
But what she doesn't realize is that they're already there.
Her parents alone do not know the cure
To reach out to their daughter who's hurt and unsure.
The things you don't know can change your whole life
I did all these things and I fought a hard fight.
I told all the lies so they would know that I hurt
But no matter the stories they stood by through the worst.
I learned the true people who would stand by my side
But I lost others too who turned away, as I numbly cried.
But I learned my lesson that had been blind to my eyes.
I put an end to my pain.
And started a new life!

Age 27

194

CHAPTER 18

My Real First Step

The next morning once I was finally released, I was still hating the world. I hated my mom for not lying to help me out. That would be the borderline in me...ahhhh one of the uniqueness of borderline is being able to switch from lawful to unlawful without even being aware. All personality for individuals with borderline happen this way. You change thoughts, actions, opinions, and even personalities to an extent, without even knowing it. Despite the drugs I did as a teenager, I had always been very lawful. This incident, and hating my mother for not lying, just further reiterated that I needed much more serious help than what my strategies could do for me. Obviously I had been trying to be successful with my own strategies for twenty-five plus years, and this is where it had gotten me. That wasn't enough for me, and my children deserved better.

As soon as I was picked up from the jail, I immediately called my mom to tell her exactly how much I hated her. Why? Because

I'm bipolar with borderline tendencies, and the anxiety of being in jail drove me to the edge, and the depression of how I was destroying my family felt like it was killing me. I just needed someone to feel as miserable as I did. Admitting you can't handle yourself alone is a very hard admission. Admitting that you will always need help is an even greater and scarier admission. Admitting that you can never be fixed makes you hate everyone.

Once I dealt with calling my superiors for damage control, my next call was to psychiatrists to make an appointment. I went to a gentleman who worked at one of the same clinics I had been to in previous years. I don't know why I picked this place because I didn't know the particular doctor, maybe just out of familiarity, I suppose. Actually I went to him because he had the soonest appointment. I knew how desperate it was for me to try again to get help! Nonetheless, this is when miracles started happening for me. I had hope that I would find a way to fix myself! NEVER again would someone else get the privilege of tucking my children in bed. I hated being away from them that night, and I would do whatever it took to ensure that it NEVER happened again. I knew it was going to be a long road, and that it wasn't be easy, but I was determined to find out what was wrong with me and fix it. My children NEEDED me to fix myself, and one night in jail taught me that life impacting lesson. My real first step was making the appointment, following through, and being honest. I wasn't completely sure I could be helped since I have never really been helped before, but this time I was going to talk even if no one would listen. I was going to find someone who would listen. I was going to talk and find someone who would listen and be able to help somehow, I prayed. I had hope so far because I was determined.

At my first visit, I did pages of assessments and diagnostic tests. I didn't mind in the least bit though because I REALLY did want to know what was wrong with me, and I NEEDED to know what to do to fix it. I had already assumed that I was bipolar, just from the research I had done on my own. Remember too, that one of the many diagnoses I had received earlier in my teenage years was also bipolar. I couldn't give any credit to that old time diagnosis though because I was never diagnosed with anything. Not to mention, at different times, they labeled me as everything, so their brief moments of considering bipolar disorder didn't mean anything to them, or me, until I learned it for myself years later.

My first assessments and tests indicated bipolar at the top of the charts, along with generalized anxiety disorder. I also flagged a high warning for borderline personality disorder, but my psychiatrist explained that the severity of it indicated on the tests was only because I was unmedicated bipolar at this point. He explained that I would have tendencies of borderline personality disorder, but that I did not necessarily exhibit all of the behaviors, psychotic or non psychotic as some borderline patients do. He explained that the borderline personality traits were only heightened because of the unmedicated bipolar and that they were minimal in comparison, so the stabilization I would reach on the bipolar disorder meds would help decrease those tendencies as well. Finding out that I also have major mood depressive disorder came as a surprise. I crashed EVEN on medications that worked, so even with my cocktail of very efficient medications, I will still always have bouts of very serious depression too: classic major mood depression disorder.

I went home feeling surprised, hopeful, and scared. I finally had a name for why I had always felt so different, and even medications to try to help with those specific problems, but how did I feel about it all, I pondered. I wasn't surprised that something was wrong with me because I already knew that and had enough people in my past meanly tell me that. I didn't know how I felt calling myself an individual with bipolar disorder, generalized anxiety disorder, and tendencies of borderline personality disorder. As I mentioned, the major mood depressive disorder wasn't discovered and diagnosed until later. I continued to occasionally deeply crash hard, despite the mood stabilizer medications that were part of my daily medication cocktails. No matter which medication we tried, these crashes continued occasionally, so we went back to the bipolar medication that worked the best for me, and added an anti depressant to combat the major mood depressive disorder. I felt scared of admitting those names to myself because it had been easier to think that I was "just fucked up" and now I had to figure out how to deal with the seriousness of the names and needs of the mental illnesses that I had. This was all only a few months after I was released from jail, and already I had found my peace of who I was, even if I was scared of what it meant. I still felt the smallest glimmer of hope.

My initial feelings for my psychiatrist were always incredible, so I need to emphasize the importance of finding a doctor, as well as a safe friend, who you can tell *everything* to if you are dealing with a mental illness. It didn't mean that everything just finally snapped into place though. We still had a lot of work to do, but he helped me reach the beginning of hope.

I have seen the same psychiatrist for two years now, and have tremendous respect for him. He listens! He understands! He doesn't try to "force a round peg into a square hole". Taking all into consideration, he is able to more effectively medicate his patients to fit their needs. He is compassionate, rough around the edges, experienced, and even a little cocky. If anyone in this world deserves to have the confidence he does though, it's him. He is a lifesaver! I know he has saved my life, among many, many others. I was only in my twenties and I had already gone incredibly far downhill. I hate to predict how my children would have come out if I hadn't gotten the help that I, and they, deserved.

No matter how wonderful he was though, it took a lot of painful truth telling and discussing for us to make any progress. In order for him to understand my needs, he had to understand me. I was just excited that he wanted to understand me. At first after the testing we discussed the results and he took the careful time to explain exactly what it meant. He carefully told me how it related to the experiences and feelings I had explained having always had. He told me how medical treatments in mental health has changed since my first experience, and even apologized for their earlier negligence with me (prior to muttering a few well-deserved curses about them under his breath). He asked me which characteristics I was feeling that day? That week? The week before? He asked so many questions. He really did seem to want to know *everything*! He asked about my appetite, sleep, and work habits. He asked about my family. We talked about so much, and I knew that he was listening. It was an actual *discussion* and I could tell that he was correctly perceiving the information I was saying. He suggested a particular medication for bipolar disorder at a minimal dosage to be increased weekly and an extended release anti-anxiety medication until I came back to see him again in two weeks (unless I needed come back sooner, of course).

Two weeks later, I walked happily, but warily, into his office. "I know it's working, but I just don't feel.......I don't feel right yet though." That was the only way I knew to describe it. Again he asked about my sleep, work, family, appetite, everything, but that didn't bother me. At least he cared enough to ask! All this after he adamantly assured me at the end of the previous session that I WASN'T CRAZY, as I had secretly thought for so many years. That reasoning and his understanding definitely made it easier to keep taking steps in the right direction. It is just so incredibly critical to have a psychiatrist and therapist, that you are comfortable with AS WELL AS a support system within family and friends if possible. Nonetheless, I seated myself in one of his oversized large padded swivel chairs, and we casually discussed how I was doing and how I was feeling with the medication and with the doses of the medication. Together we agreed to increase the medication that was targeted for my bipolar disorder, as well as add something for anxiety induced insomnia. I was up to three pills daily, a little intimidated by it all still, but for the first time ever I actually believed that it was going to be ok. The medications hadn't made a huge difference, but enough to keep me coming back and enough to prove to myself that I was coming closer and closer to the New Beginning that I had wanted for so long. As scheduled, I was back two weeks later. We had started a positive doctor and patient relationship: I had HOPE!

Over the course of the next few visits, we continued to slightly increase the doses until I felt comfortable. What?!?! Me?!?!

Comfortable?!?! I couldn't believe it. Yes, it had taken a while to get the medications and foundation with my doctor stable, so it wasn't an immediate feeling of relief, but overtime it did happen. I was able to let my guard up a little because more and more I just felt comfortable and "normal." That word always held so much power to me because I had always felt that it represented everything that I could never be. I had spent more than twenty-five years trying to perfect strategies at covering up and disguising mental illness, and it didn't work and I was miserable anyways. Had I known that this could be how life felt all along, I would've gone door to door until I found a doctor that I was comfortable with instead of just trying to handle it myself (which obviously had never turned out too well for me in the past).

I will always have to go to my psychiatrist because I cannot be cured. I can accept that now though because my medications keep my roller coaster stable enough that it doesn't change who I am or how I live my life. It doesn't put me in the depths of hell when I'm severely low and depressed, and it helps me refrain from the highs of manic mistakes that usually end with regret. Its just another appointment that I go to, but that doesn't make me any different than anyone else. It's just a repertoire of medications that other people may not have to take, but also similar to the regiment of medications that people with physical illnesses have too. Besides, who the hell cares if I can be cured or not if you are able to make me feel "normal?"

Does this mean that all bundled together it has made my life easier? Not necessarily. That is why I emphasize that all the pieces of the puzzle need to be in place; comfort with past and present, family and friends support structure, correct diagnosis, medications and therapy, grieving hopefully followed by self acceptance, and an inner peace with who you are and the positive impact that you have if you choose to. Hell no, it hasn't made my life altogether easier. I still have my occasional bipolar crashes, but I also have a support system now for how get help with coping, since my obvious earlier alternatives weren't very helpful. Now when I feel that I am at the beginning of a crash I call my aunt (family support) and psychiatrist (medical support), and somehow am always able to get through it. It still hurts like hell, but no matter how low it gets anymore, I never go as low as I EVER did in the past, and I have HOPE.

In order to give credit where credit is due, the therapist I had as a teenager worked hard with me, and helped me tremendously. I don't think either of us really realized it then, but as an adult I am able to reflect back and realize the help I received from our therapy together. Her tremendous efforts with me made it so that I did not have to extensively deal with some of the big issues in my life that could have contributed to an even more complex diagnosis as an adult. We all know that when problems are put off, they only get worse. I apply the same theory to my time spent with my therapist when I was younger. She was one of the people who helped me deal with the times I was a victim. She worked through that with me. She helped me deal with my traumas and losses, and helped me move beyond grieving and accepting. It wasn't until I was an adult and mature enough to realize it. She was one of the people who helped to instill a sense of inner peace with all of the things I have been through and then try to mold it into something positive, that hopefully can positively impact others. My miracle psychiatrist who I see currently is a miracle, but he had a "wingman" who helped to set the stage for later success too.

Since I was exposed early to mental illness (at age thirteen) I have learned a lot about it in my journey. It seems like I spent the first twenty plus years learning how to disguise it, and the last most recent years learning how to deal with it and use my experiences and understandings to help others. I could never have gotten to the place that I am without my bundle of experiences, and guess what? For now, I am happy with where I am! Horrible shit happens, and people have mental illnesses that require a lifelong commitment to a list of medications, BUT GOOD THINGS CAN ALWAYS STILL COME FROM IT! Circumstances, mental illnesses, and happenstance bad shit doesn't guarantee that a person can't feel better, and even happy, and it took me more than twenty years to learn that.

Truthfulness is so important. It is crucial to be truthful with yourself, trusted friends and family, and especially with psychiatrists and therapists. Sometimes individuals with Borderline personality disorder find the concept of "truthfulness" difficult because depending on the phase, everything you think can literally feel like the truth. Even only having tendencies of the disorder, I have been able to recognize that in myself. So, what do I do? I call my aunt and tell her to watch me for any warning signs; refusal to answer the phone, avoidance of typical activities, depression, etc. She has had to learn a lot to be able to help me, but again, the need for a support structure is definite if it is possible. Bipolar disorder makes truthfulness hard too because it is easy to tell the truth once we are out of mania or out of our lows, but it is often times too hard to admit it to anyone when you are actually experiencing it. I don't have a complete understanding of why these mental illnesses twist themselves so much with the concept of truthfulness, but I do know that it is key in helping to learn to make yourself feel better. You have to be truthful.

Learn the habits of your cycles, the triggers (if any) and reflect. Everyone has to make mistakes to learn, so don't over criticize, but be sure to learn. I still screw up along my way in dealing with the real world intertwined with having mental illnesses, but guilt and regret can eat away at your heart and soul. You have to move on, hang on, and don't let go no matter what. Easier said than done, I know, but surprisingly enough to me, while working with my team of supporters I actually learned that it does get easier. It honestly does. Don't let go! I have even had to adjust and increase my meds quite a bit over the time my Doctor and I have worked together, and had to conquer some difficult side effects, but recovery and hope is worth it.

Disguises and all, if you had asked me on any given day if I was overall happy in the past twenty-five years, I would've at least hesitated, if not said no. If you asked me in the past two years and even now if I am overall happy (even on a bad day) I can think "DON'T LET GO" and I won't even blink an eye without a truthful answer "YES I AM HAPPY!

Memorable Moments

When I was four, my parents also took me to Disney World. This was a vacation before my brother was born, so I was spoiled rotten and got nearly everything that I wanted, as if the trip alone wasn't enough. I wasn't a greedy spoiled child, but I sure did get what I wanted pretty often.

I was amazed at the characters I saw walking freely around the park. I eagerly smiled for pictures with Mickey Mouse, Minnie, Goofy, and every other Disney character I could find. I loved the Dumbo ride, the carousel, and the Haunter Mansion. I rode the rides until we were all practically ill from all the twirling and bumping around. The park was so big that I know we didn't even cover a fraction of it, but it was pure Heaven to a child.

We even stayed for the torchlight parade. The only words I can think of to describe how I felt during that time is magical. As the sparkling lights reflected in my young excited eyes, it created moments I will never forget.

What We Learn as a Child

As a child we learn what we need to know.
As a child we learn that milk makes strong bones.
As a child we learn to be friendly and share.
We learn to be careful and not to pull hair.
As a child you learn "don't ever bite,
try getting along, and never start fights."
As a child we learn to say "thank you" and "please."
We learn that band aids cure the scrapes on our knees.
As a child we learn good things we can do to make a change,
But it's too bad some people didn't learn it that way

Age 17

CHAPTER 19

My New Beginning

I always got nervous right before school started, and I probably always will. When I was a child, meeting my teacher was so intimidating because I was so short and they seemed to much taller, bigger, and perfect. Although I had both good and bad teachers, throughout my younger years I couldn't help but look up to them. There was just something about elementary school teachers! When I was in elementary school they were just viewed as heroes.

Not much has changed in the past twenty years as far as that is concerned because my students also look at me as one of their heroes, but I still get intimidated before school starts when I have to meet their parents. I just hope each year that I will live up to the parents' expectations since I consider working with their children to be such a privilege. Once alone in the classroom with my kids my soul guides my teaching, as teaching is what I was meant to do. How lucky am I that I get to go to work every morning to a job that I love? Each day is different. Each child touches a different part of my heart. I can relate to some. I encourage and support the ones who struggle. I challenge the ones who are bored and above regular learning standards. I want more than to teach them. I want to *reach* them. I don't ever want them to ever feel like I did in school so I hope to be a link for students who might have otherwise fallen through the cracks. Already I can think of several children who I have bonded with in that nature because they continually come back to visit me. They come by, even years later, for advice, help, encouragement, support, and good books since reading is one of my passions and I instill that in many of my children. I tell my students that we are a class family and that I do love them and that they will always be a part of my family because I will be here for them. I remind them that if there is anything they ever need, all they need to do is ask me. I also convince the parents of the same. Teaching is so special to me, so I really take it as a hugh warm-hearted responsibility.

In addition to helping students progress as far as they can as learners, I am more able to efficiently teach them that we are all different, and that we all have different needs. I teach that fair is what someone needs to be successful, and not necessarily the same for all people. I teach tolerance and acceptance. I teach empathy and compassion. I have formed the most special and unique bonds with my students. I try to help each one of them in the way that they appear to need help. I remember my experiences in school, and try to better myself so that they don't fall through the emotional or academic cracks. I talk to them, but I listen, and respond in the most heart felt way that I can. They may only be children, but they will remember and grow into adults. Maybe in the year I have them, I can better the world one child at a time. Maybe all I am meant for is to help just one person, but if I can even help one as a result of my experiences and learning, then I have made the positive difference I strive to make. I already feel success with my life, but that will never stop me from trying to always improve and learn.

I earned my bachelors degree in elementary education and my masters degree in varying exceptionalities (special education in all areas). I have been teaching for several years now, and my understanding of my experiences and journey has now come full circle. I realized that I have finally reached my New Beginning. It wasn't teaching that did it, but I wouldn't have been nearly as good and compassionate of a teacher without my background, however good or bad it may have been. Teaching helped me hang on for one more day sometimes. I always loved it, but having learned what I learned about mental illnesses and my own acceptance and recovery, it has made me even more of a better teacher. Even when I feel like I can't help myself, I can still always help someone else somehow.

I have been nominated several times for prestigious awards for my excellence in teaching. I have won awards for my success in teaching to meet the diverse needs of learners. I have presented instruction and taught classes for other teachers in attempt to help them better their own teaching. I have been selected as an elite few to receive specialized training to implement, and then present and guide other teachers to adopt some of the strategies I have learned and taught. For years now, my test scores at the end of the year have served as very strong documentation of my effectiveness as a teacher. I am recognized on a National level for my performance as a teacher, as to opposed to only being certified in the state where I live. Moreover and most importantly I have reached many lives, in part, due to the horrible history I had to endure to make it to this point.

Remember there is always an ending, and always the hope offered by a New Beginning. I couldn't be the person I am without my past. My past led me to my New Beginning; to the recovery, peace, normalcy…and hope that I had always been seeking. Altogether the best part of new beginnings. Hope! I couldn't have reached my New Beginning without accepting mental illness, seeking treatment, following, accepting, and using treatment suggestions, seeing my therapist and psychiatrist on a regular basis, and following through with their medication regiment. I have a New Beginning now because I was willing to let go of the mistakes of my past, and begin the medicated hopeful beginning of the next stage in my life.

In my heart, and also verified in all the letters and pictures I continually receive in the mail, I have touched hearts and lives, and will never be forgotten. I may have several mental illnesses, but I didn't let go. I found my New Beginning, at last, and I AM HAPPY! Mental illness doesn't diminish me or define who I am. I do. The definition of me is by my own choice! I am a happy individual who endured a long road, a mother of two, a teacher, and a love of life…and only by the way, I happen to have a mental illness that makes me stronger because it makes me see the world in more views than most people. I am able to be more stable and compassionate as a result. I didn't let go!

Memorable Moments

My son was adopted after having endured many negative life altering situations. He definitely had his own issues by the time I adopted him. We spent years in therapy. I tried everything I could think of to break through his tough exterior and help him. His behaviors were beyond aggressive, and he was always in trouble at home and at school. I even had specific testing done on him to see if there was a problem that the schools or I could help him with. We found nothing, other than the possibility that he could be emotionally handicapped, but was too young to be certain. My heart broke, as I envisioned him having to endure the battles that I had to face.

After first grade, and many tough times with him, I decided it was time to pursue psychiatry since that was the only avenue I hadn't tried yet. His ADD and ADHD were becoming increasingly obvious, so I wanted to be able to give him all the help I could if this was, in fact, the problem.

The Doctor agreed it was a possibility, so we decided to try a medication. I asked Taylor about two weeks after he had been on the medication how it made him feel. I had certainly noticed a positive difference, but wanted to see what his opinion was too. He looked deeply into my eyes, and said, "It makes me feel like I'm not a bad kid anymore. My brain doesn't feel like it always makes me get in trouble anymore and I like being me now."

I ensured that my son didn't fall through the cracks, for now, like I did so many years ago. That was one moment that I will never forget.

New Beginning

I have my health.
I have my life.
I've had hardships,
but I've still survived
I've been abused and hurt.
I feel like my life's been the worst.
I've felt lost and alone.
But I finally feel peace; like I'm at home
I will continue to cry at times
I will continue to climb to new heights
But hope holds me stable
Because I know I am always able
to

not let go!

Age 28

CHAPTER 20

So Where Does That Leave Me Now?

I attended, and still do attend, therapy to help work through the borderline personality tendencies. Since they were minimal with my bipolar disorder medication to begin with, I didn't have to fight this fight as hard as other people may. I learned that it is okay to feel the way that I have always felt. That made me feel so much better, as opposed to always secretly feeling that I was crazy. I'm sure each therapist works with each patient in a different way, but my therapist talked to me openly about how I felt, so it only encouraged me to talk more openly as well. We both can easily recognize how much progress I have made by sticking to the right treatment plan. Is it easy? Never. I don't think it's ever easy telling someone the secrets and skeletons of your closet, but that's why I emphasized the importance of having someone you are comfortable with and complete honesty. The borderline tendencies were more easily resolved for me the more we seemed to get the generalized anxiety disorder, major mood depressive disorder, and bipolar disorder medically under control. My therapist also helped me get my anorexia and bulimia under control too so that I have also reached recovery in those areas as well.

In reference to the generalized anxiety disorder, major mood depressive disorder, and bipolar disorder, they seem to be interwoven together. I have a cocktail of medications that I take daily for each. I have a treatment plan, and psychiatrist. I can happily say that I have recovered so much already that I only need to see my therapist infrequently every six to eight weeks. I have accepted the illnesses, learned a lot in the process, and have recovered so much. It is true that I can not reach recovery from bipolar disorder, generalized anxiety disorder, and major mood depressive disorder without medications, but I have reached recovery by what began as simply seeking help. I cannot even begin to explain the difference and positive impact it has had on my life. Of course, the old adage is true, "the more you put into it, the more you get out of it," but if you are honest with yourself and your supporters, recovery is possible! Don't ever give up on that hope.

I am still a teacher, who inspires to improve myself each and every year. I strive to be a lifelong learner, and I am blessed go to a job that I love and come home to two wonderful children. I am happy with myself. I will always have to see a psychiatrist for medications, and I still have to "tweak" my medications sometimes, but never for a second have I regretted my decision to strive for recovery. I now have a very simplistic view of mental illness. People wouldn't deprive a person suffering from a physical illness such as diabetes, cancer, or other illnesses from the medications that their bodies need. With that in mind, people with mental illnesses shouldn't be deprived the medications their bodies need.

I hope to continue to teach and reach as many children as I can, but I also hope to stand up for individuals with mental illnesses. I'm just one person though, so I don't know how much of a change I can make, but that certainly won't stop me from trying. I want to change how people view individuals with mental illnesses. I want to help encourage those with mental illnesses to seek help. I want supporters of individuals with mental illness to understand. I don't know how much power of effectiveness I could ever have with this endeavor, but I am taking a stand that mental illness is there, real, often painful, and should be respected as other illnesses would be. I want to reach all people with the teaching that people with mental illness can recover, be happy, and be even more successful than individuals without mental illnesses because we have seen and endured more than one side of life. We have walked a mile certainly in more than just one pair of moccasins. Don't forget that can be an asset to life. Take a stand! For yourself! You are not any lesser of a person if you have a mental illness!

It may never be easy, and it takes time and patience to find the right people to work with, the right treatment plan, and the correct medications and dosages, but it is definitely worth the wait. It is worth the struggles it takes to finally get there. I can write about mental illness compassionately because I have suffered from it, destroyed parts of my life as a result, fallen to the depths of despair, and have lived to recover. I recognize my strengths in my mental illness, and I would've never thought that it could turn out to be a strength. It did though because I held on through the long and painful journey, recovered,

and **didn't let go**

Originally I wrote this poem for my beloved granny. When she passed away, in my heart, it always stood out as my tribute to her. I believe she would be pleased with where I am in my life right now, and would be thrilled to share her poem as a tribute to my family for helping me to come so far. What was once titled "My Granny" has been altered to show the depth of love and respect I feel for my family in a variation newly titled "My Family"

My Family

They taught me to love.
They taught me to care.
They said, if you need me,"
"I'll always be there."
<u>You're the best of them all!</u>
<u>And I'd just like to say,</u>
<u>that I'll always love and thank you</u>
<u>in every way!</u>

Ages 16 and 29

EPILOGUE

The Hope of a Healthy Life
After a New Beginning

$\mathscr{I}$ did foreclose on the home I co-owned with Ryan. I did reach financial bottom. I lost everything I had, which wasn't necessarily much to begin with, but I did reach the bottom. We attempted to do a "short sale" instead of having to foreclose, but the mortgage company refused the offer. Technically the process we pursued was called a deid in lieu of foreclosure, but it is nearly the same thing. I hit the depths of the bottom of my marriage when I got divorced. I left scarred and scared with two children to solely support. My mind was racing, depressed, and screaming for help, but who was I supposed to turn to? My kids? I didn't even have enough money to pay for school lunches at the time, so fortunately the co workers at my school and pitched in so that my son would be able to get his lunches at our school without it having to break the bank for me. At this point, my "money tree" had died and shriveled up, and I had no home to call my own, no money, and no support. Rock bottom!

Emotionally, although I hung on by a thread for a long time, I was a wreck. I made a mental list of to do things: 1. finalize the divorce, 2. finalize the process with the home we had to foreclose on, 3. tackle the increasingly noticeable special needs of my son, and 4. take care of my emotional needs. Little did I know that my carefully structured plans for recovery would greatly falter as the needs rearranged themselves when I was arrested.

The night I spent in jail was a pivotal turning point. I didn't sleep that night. I knew where my life was going if I didn't intervene NOW and stop the cycle. I began to make "fixing" myself my first priority as I sat there in a cold, darkened, damp jail cell thinking of my children being read their bedtime story by someone else, being tucked in by someone else, waking up to someone else…I just couldn't imagine the rest of my life feeling as miserable as I always had. I couldn't stand the thought of having to keep up the disguises, and failing at it every now and then, for the rest of my entire life. When I was younger, it was my mom who was smart enough to realize that someone had to intervene. This time it was ME who decided that it was finally time to really intervene, and for me to accept the help! Mental illness treatment always has to be a priority, and that lesson, I did have to learn the hard way.

Honestly, I couldn't bear the thought of life being this hard forever, so I had to either get help or kill myself because I just couldn't handle it. Thankfully, I found the one thing that kept me wanting to be alive; my beautiful children. The two precious beautiful babies NEEDED me and I NEEDED them, so I knew it was time to begin recovering. I had already crashed, fallen, burned, and hit rock bottom. All that was left to do was pick up the pieces of the puzzle and start over. So I did. I began sessions with my psychiatrist, began a medication regiment, accepted and learned about my mental illnesses, began to more carefully monitor my moods and feelings, and just do the damn best that I can.

Since working so closely with my psychiatrist and hitting rock bottom before I came nearly crawling to him, no matter how many times we may have to "tweak" my medications, my emotions no longer get the better of me. I am balanced. I feel "normal." Even in my lowest of lows, there is HOPE that I will eventually feel better. In my highest of highs, there is always HOPE that I am becoming an even better person than I already believe that I am. No matter which personality seems to be potentially interfering the most, they are at peace, and there is HOPE that I will continue to move forward in a positive direction as I have been. No matter what anxiety I am feeling, there in HOPE that "this too shall pass." HOPE! I reached the bottom, and then found my New Beginning; I found the HOPE that is offered by New Beginnings, and it saved my life.

As you well know by now, my life hasn't always been easy, but I have used it to the best of my capabilities to be the person I have wanted to become. Accepting my mental illnesses wasn't easy, because I knew I was intelligent enough to use strategies and coping methods. The problem is, no matter how successful these strategies were at disguising myself, they were never enough to make me happy. My advice to individuals dealing with mental illness is to accept you for who you are. There is a certain beauty to being different. In cases such as mine, it may take twenty years to find it. I suppose it could take even more or less, but acceptance of your strengths and weaknesses is so important.

Even once you have been successful at finding a psychiatrist and therapist that you are comfortable with, continue to be truthful with yourself and them, as well as a family or friend who can be trusted enough to help you when you crash. My family has spent nearly thirty years helping me pick up my puzzle pieces as they scattered, and I don't know what I would've done without them.

Yes, despite medication, you will still crash. You will still experience mania too, but the good promise of the right treatment plan is that it minimizes the highs and lows and makes the ride of the roller coaster more enjoyable and tolerable. And lastly, **don't ever let go**! There is *always* hope!